PICKUPS

PICKUPS

THE PHENOMENAL MAINSTAY OF AMERICA'S AUTOMOBILE INDUSTRY

TERRY JACKSON

CHARTWELL
BOOKS, INC.

A QUINTET BOOK

Published by Chartwell Books, Inc.
A Division of Book Sales, Inc.
114 Northfield Avenue
Edison, New Jersey 08837

This edition produced for sale in the U.S.A., its territories and dependencies only.

ISBN 0-7858-0615-6

CREATIVE DIRECTOR: *Richard Dewing*
ART DIRECTOR: *Patrick Carpenter*
DESIGNER: *Simon Balley*
SENIOR EDITOR: *Anna Briffa*
EDITOR: *Kit Coppard*

Typeset in Great Britain by
Central Southern Typesetters, Eastbourne
Manufactured in China by
Regent Publishing Services Ltd
Printed in China by
Leefung-Asco Printers Ltd

DEDICATION:
For my sister Kathie Powell and her family, who appreciate
the ruggedness of a good pickup truck.

contents

Picture this scene: the year is around 1900 in the American West. It's just after sun-up and a farmer is leaving his rough, three-room house and heading for the barn. He's going to make a 10-mile trip into the nearest town for some supplies.

He needs seeds, a few tools, some fencing wire – and then head out into his fields to do some work before nightfall. In the barn he passes the upholstered buggy that he and his family hitch up to the mare for their every-Sunday trip to church and stops in front of a wooden, flatbed wagon. Little more than a 10-by-15-foot set of boards with 18-inch high siderails mounted to four huge wooden-spoked, metal-banded wheels, the conveyance is known as a "buckboard" – a reference to the way it moves over the rutted frontier paths. There's a hitch at the front for a single horse or a two-horse team, and the driver directs the animals with reins while seated on a rough, raised plank mounted at the front of the wagon.

The buckboard is as utilitarian as its description. The farmer will hitch up his horse and take a swift but hardly comfortable ride to wherever he needs to go. He will routinely throw in the cargo bed items ranging from foodstuffs to dirt-encrusted tools to sharp-edged fence posts. He'll drive the buckboard over rugged, rocky terrain, through streams and mud bogs – just about anywhere a horse will go. If the wheels become scarred, the floorboards gouged and splintered – so what? This vehicle isn't supposed to look good – it's built for work! If something more stylish and comfortable is called for, then there's the upholstered buggy, with its springy ride and fringed canopy that keeps the rain and sun off its occupants.

On his way into town the farmer and his buckboard encounter one of the new century's marvels.

The farmer pulls back on the reins of his mare and the buckboard slows as it comes to a rise in the road. He can't see what's coming yet, but up ahead he hears an unfamiliar cacophony of bangs and rattles. His horse snorts and rears slightly as a smell of hot metal and oil is carried toward them on the breeze.

As the farmer crests the rise, he sees the strange contraption: it has four wheels like his buckboard and his buggy back home, but it's moving under its own power – without a horse! A stranger is sitting on an upholstered seat, dressed in a full-length coat known as a duster, a pair of goggles clamped over his eyes. The vehicle bobs and weaves over the deep ruts in the road and the driver wrestles with a steering bar for control. A cloud of smoke streams from the back of the vehicle and every so often there's a loud bang and the exhaust smoke increases.

The farmer holds tight to his reins, moves over to let the vehicle pass, and tips his hat to the driver. As they come side-by-side, the farmer stares intently and realizes this must be one of those automobiles he read about in the newspaper a while back. All the rage in the city, the paper said. "Huh," thought the farmer, "a toy with absolutely no use for folks who have to do real work for a living."

Of course, history was to prove the farmer wrong. But he was right in thinking the first automobiles were no substitute for his buckboard or for any other turn-of-the-century vehicle that was used for hauling heavy and bulky items.

The early automobiles were first and foremost pleasure vehicles, best suited for city use by wealthier people. Photographs of street scenes from the early 1900s show automobiles coexisting with trolleys and horse-drawn delivery vehicles. Out in the country, however, the horse and wagon were staples of farm and ranch life.

It would be years after the first cars were built before the automotive family tree would branch out into trucks and then into what we know today as the light-duty truck, or, more familiarly, the pickup. Such a slow beginning is hard to imagine, given the way the pickup has become such an integral part of transportation for tens of millions of families.

How popular is the pickup? Well, the top-selling vehicles in the United States are not cars but the Ford F150 and the Chevrolet C/K series pickups — and they've held those top positions for 14 years. Add the compact Ford Ranger, and trucks occupy three of the top five annual sales positions. Overall, trucks account for 40 percent of the market. The Chevrolet and the GMC truck divisions of General Motors sell more teal-colored pickups in a given year than the entire Buick division sells cars of all colors. Since the end of World War II, pickup truck sales worldwide have grown at a rate that outpaces any other single type of vehicle, and the trend continues. Some analysts believe that trucks will account for 50 per cent of all new-vehicle sales worldwide by the year 2005.

Not even the farmer's horse-drawn buckboard ever enjoyed such a central place in the world of transportation.

Compared with the rapid acceptance of the automobile, the love affair with the truck was slow to develop. While the passenger car had an aura of glamor and sophistication, when it came to tucks, practicality won out over considerations of fashion or technical innovation.

At the start of the 20th century, American railroads did virtually all the cross-country hauling of goods. For local haulage, a horse and wagon provided cheap delivery in the cities, and was often the only way to do heavy hauling in the country, where paved

ABOVE This 1917 Ford light-duty truck was typical of early pickups. Essentially it was a Model T sedan with a truck body grafted onto the back.

roads were nonexistent. It was only when the spread of the passenger automobile prompted governments to build paved roads connecting cities and rural areas that the value of a motorized cargo vehicle became impossible to ignore.

Although history records the first appearance of commercially available automobiles with a certain accuracy, the history of the first trucks is much less clear. In the United States, one of the first trucks to be built came out of the Winton Company of Cleveland, Ohio, in 1898. A modified car, it could carry only a very limited amount of cargo, and only a few were built. Other companies made similar half-hearted attempts at truck-building, including some trucks that were propelled by electric motors or steam engines, such as the White two-cylinder steam-powered delivery vehicles built in 1901. In Europe, the world's first gasoline-powered commercial vehicle had been produced by Panhard et Levassor in 1893. And, perhaps because in Europe there were more paved roads available in cities and the countryside than in the United States, other European companies such as Peugeot, Benz and Daimler, soon offered a variety of gasoline-powered cargo vehicles.

When trucks did grab hold in the United States, starting in about 1910, for the most part they were large, rough-hewn vehicles designed solely with heavy-duty work in mind. Companies like Diamond T, Reo, White, Autocar, International and Mack were the dominant players in the truck market. Often, what these companies built weren't even complete vehicles. Mack, for example, opened a factory in 1905 in Allentown, PA, which turned out a large truck chassis that the buyer would then have fitted with a cargo bed or enclosed cab by another manufacturer, such as Fruehauf and Heil. A typical vehicle might have a carrying capacity of five tons and a top speed of 20 mph.

It's not as though the big car manufacturers of the day were completely unaware of the market for trucks: Ford offered its first purpose-built truck in 1905 and called it a Delivery Car. It cost $950, and just 10 were built. The truck market started off small. There was such a huge demand for Henry Ford's Model T automobile and the passenger cars produced by both Chevrolet and the Dodge Brothers that their production capacity was entirely eaten up, leaving little time for anything else. Simply put, Ford and the others didn't need the truck business in the beginning.

RIGHT Like most early pickups, this 1917 Dodge is likely to have come from the factory without a body and this wire-mesh cargo body would have been added by the purchaser.

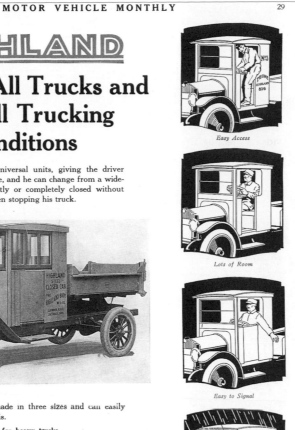

Slowly, trucks began to take hold and push out the horse-drawn wagon. Pavement started reaching out to all parts of the country, spurred by the growth in private automobile ownership. Trucks followed along, mostly as commercial delivery vehicles or construction and farm workhorses.

As the 1920s approached, car manufacturers began to take renewed interest in the truck market. Although they, too, would produce the large, long-haul trucks that would evolve into today's tractor-trailer rigs, Ford, Chevrolet and Dodge started to carve out a niche that was being neglected by the dedicated commercial truck builders – the small utility truck that we know today as the pickup.

In 1912, Ford reintroduced the Delivery Car that it first offered in 1905, using an advertising campaign that said it was a car that "delivered the goods." There had been other Ford trucks before then, but all had been passenger cars that were sold as automobiles and then converted by other companies into trucks. The model that Ford delivered in 1912 was much the same – a standard 22hp Model T with an enclosed delivery body on the back. Cost was

between $590 and $700, and it remained virtually unchanged until 1925. Primary customers included city department stores and other dry-goods delivery operations. Few found their way initially into use by private citizens.

Chevrolet joined the light-truck market in 1918 with its Model 490. This was a half-ton-capacity truck that was based on a passenger car chassis. Like many of the early trucks, it was delivered with just a driver's cowl and fenders, and the buyer was then expected to install whatever cargo body they needed. A larger, one-ton version – dubbed, curiously, the Model T, with no apparent objection from Ford – was based on a true truck chassis and also was offered without body.

In 1917 Dodge entered the fray with a light-duty truck of its own that first found its way to market as an American ambulance shipped overseas during World War I. The civilian version was called the Screenside, and, like its Chevy and Ford counterparts, was based on a passenger car chassis. Unlike Chevrolet, however, Dodge offered its first truck as a complete vehicle.

ABOVE *An advertisement for the Highland Body Manufacturing Company shows how light-duty trucks were first marketed. A manufacturer would sell a base chassis and companies like Highland would attach a special-use body.*

ABOVE *The exact origin of this 1920s-vintage Model T is difficult to determine. It could originally have been a pickup, but more likely it was a sedan that was later converted.*

Other manufacturers, such as Studebaker, International and Willys-Overland, also began producing light trucks, and, like the models being churned out by Ford, Chevy, and Dodge, almost all of them wound up in commercial service. Despite their being smaller and more driver-friendly than their giant heavy-duty cousins, these trucks were, however, still an evolutionary step or two from what would eventually become the first genuine pickup.

Given all the aftermarket truck-body makers that were in business from the 1900s through the 1920s, it's difficult to pinpoint exactly when the first factory-built pickup made its appearance. Arguably, the honor should go to Ford, which in 1925 took a Model T roadster, chopped off the back part of the bodywork and installed a very short open cargo bed. With minor exceptions the Model T was barely changed from its admittedly rugged passenger car counterpart.

RIGHT *Small businesses and farms were the primary customers for light-duty trucks before World War II, as this advertisement for a 1928 Chevrolet shows.*

Not to be left behind, Chevrolet followed with a similar model in 1926 that was either a standard coupé or roadster with the back end chopped off and a cargo bed installed. As with Ford, pickup sales were small compared to car and heavy-duty truck sales, but were encouraging enough for Chevrolet to keep revising and upgrading the pickup as the years passed.

The term pickup (spelled at first with a hyphen) didn't come into widespread use until the 1930s. Until then, names such as "express delivery" or "delivery car" were used by the manufacturers. Exactly where the name came from is a mystery, but in all likelihood was coined in some long-forgotten advertising copy that in turn probably got the term from the owners of the trucks themselves. They weren't trucks for long-distance hauling: they were used just for picking something up at one location and delivering it to some place else in the locality.

Jaunty in overall looks, the first pickups were the perfect solution for the small-business person who needed some cargo capacity, but also wanted a comfortable vehicle. They were rugged enough for country work, yet small and maneuverable enough to cope with city traffic. In hindsight, the creation of the pickup truck seems a stunningly good idea. In reality, it was born in the boom times of the 1920s, when

there was a market for just about anything with a gasoline engine and four wheels. Heavier, larger-capacity trucks at first outsold pickups by a 10-to-1 margin, so pickups in the beginning were by no means an instant success. Perhaps the first true niche vehicle, it's doubtful that car makers back then could have imagined that the pickup would become a staple of American life 70 years later.

With the great stock market crash of 1929 and the subsequent Depression, truck sales became more vital to manufacturers, given that many people could no longer afford to buy new cars. Sales to farmers, small businesses and government agencies helped keep them afloat. At Ford, for example, truck sales had peaked in 1929 and would not regain that total for near 20 years. During this period, the pickup truck remained largely a no-frills light-delivery vehicle that also did a lot of the dirty work at construction and farm sites – although in the depths of the Depression thousands of destitute farmers had to resort to the horse-drawn buckboards.

As the nation came out of the Depression, cars started to become more stylish, and so did the pickup truck. In the late 1930s manufacturers resorted to styling cues that made pickups seem more like their huge commercial counterparts –

ABOVE *Pneumatic tires, flowing front fenders, and sturdier cabs were the trends that began to appear on pickups in the 1930s.*

LEFT *This 1935 Dodge KC pickup was a part of the styling era that would evolve into the pickup trucks that we know today. This truck came off the assembly line as a complete unit, and had many of the same features as a regular car. This truck sports a two-tone paint scheme.*

BELOW *This 1928 Chevrolet one-ton truck came with an enclosed cab for an extra $115. This rear view shows the complete enclosure and conveniently placed window light. This particular truck was finished in Biscaye Green Duco, striped in gold.*

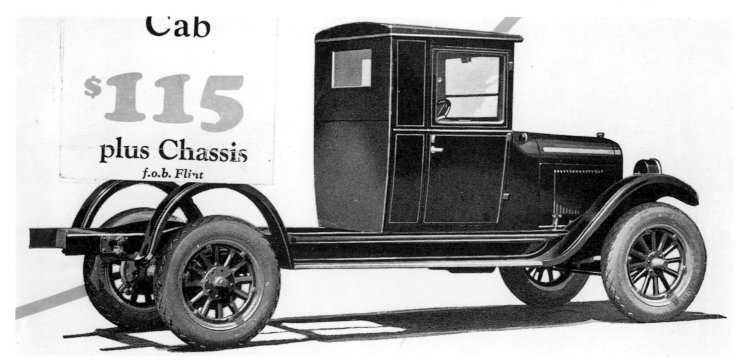

large, dominant grilles at the front, combined with bulbous fenders. The restyled 1936–8 Chevrolet and GMC trucks were good examples of this, as were the Fords of the same years. Although designers were paying close attention to how people wanted their trucks to look, there was still little doubt that these vehicles were meant for work. Some passenger car niceties were often overlooked. On the 1937 Chevrolet, to cite one extreme example, the gas tank was located underneath the passenger's seat, and the seat cushion had to be pulled up to gain access to the tank to put in fuel. Fortunately, the situation was remedied the next year when the tank-filler neck was routed to a cap mounted on the outside door pillar.

One of the most stylish pre-World War II pickups was the 1940–1 Ford, which marked a turn back toward linking the styling of the pickup truck with the current passenger car model. Looks were deceptive, however. Although the 1940 Ford cars and pickups looked identical at the front, only the small chrome grille was interchangeable. The fenders on the truck were tapered differently at the back to blend with the more slab-sided doors used on the pickups. Also, the

pickups rode on a modified car chassis that used heavier-gauge steel.

Chevrolet's pickups borrowed heavily from what we now know as the art deco movement. The heavy chrome bars used on the front of its 1941 truck could (with a little imagination) be said to resemble a cityscape of straight skyscrapers. Unlike Ford, however, Chevrolet – which held a slight sales edge over Ford most years – kept a number of significant big-truck themes on its pickups, such as the two-pane V-shaped front windshield that opened at the bottom to allow ventilation.

In other ways, such as rubber floor mats, no sound-deadening and rough-riding suspensions, these pickups were still quite different from automobiles. Still, some car influences could be found, particularly on the growing list of options that allowed buyers to slightly customize their trucks. Chrome trim, such as shiny front bumpers and the bezels around the headlights, were options, as were cab heaters and other so-called frills. As the way people thought of pickup trucks began to change, so too did their impact on the overall truck market. In 1937, for example, more

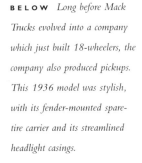

BELOW Long before Mack Trucks evolved into a company which just built 18-wheelers, the company also produced pickups. This 1936 model was stylish, with its fender-mounted spare-tire carrier and its streamlined headlight casings.

LEFT *Optional on the 1940 Ford were white wall tires and chrome grille trim, as well as a chrome bumper.*

than 600,000 new trucks were sold. While the big rigs sold by Mack, Reo and Diamond T are lumped into that total, trucks sold by Ford, Chevrolet and Dodge – which primarily produced light-duty pickups – accounted for more than half that total. Nonetheless, the pickup truck was still mainly a country workhorse, rarely seen in the more urban areas, where consumers still preferred the passenger car.

Development of the pickup – and of the automobile in general – was put on hold with America's entry into world war II in December 1941. All Detroit factories were put on a war-production footing and the manufacture of military vehicles became the priority. Light-duty trucks became troop carriers and jeeps (the term deriving from the initials GP, for "general-purpose" vehicles), and until 1945 there were no new pickups built for civilians. When new trucks began rolling off the assembly line in 1945 and 1946, they were at first the same models that had been new in 1941 and for the subsequent four years had been pressed into military service.

But the United States that emerged after World War II was a vastly different country. And while the immediate, pent-up demand for trucks and cars meant that just about anything coming off the assembly line had an eager buyer, what consumers wanted in their new vehicles – particularly in their pickups – dictated some basic changes.

UNDER THE HOOD

Given that some of the earliest of pickups were derived from passenger cars, it followed that the engines in both were very similar. Soon, however, pickup buyers began to demand larger engines with more torque to better handle the delivery and industrial uses that the first pickups were put to.

While huge six-cylinder engines – and some V-8 diesels – were developed from the start for the large, commercial trucks that would eventually become what we know today as the semi-tractor-trailer rig, the four-cylinder engine was the powerplant found in most pickups at first. Although a few utilitarian trucks, such as the 1914 International Auto Wagon, had two-cylinder engines, the Ford Model T's engine was typical of the day.

It was a 177 cu. in. L-shaped cylinder-head design that had a compression ratio of just 4.5 to 1 and developed a modest 20 hp. That seems ludicrously feeble these days for a motor vehicle of any sort, but the Model T engine was not only reliable but developed its maximum power at just 1400 rpm, giving good low-end torque. Farmers often used their Ford trucks and cars to pull up dead tree stumps, a testament to the ability of the gutsy Model T four.

The engine in Chevrolet's 1918 Model 490 also had four cylinders and developed 20hp. Where Chevrolet was able to claim some marginal advantage

was how it delivered those 20 horses to the rear wheels. It used a worm-drive reduction-gear setup that gave superior pulling power to the ring-and-pinion arrangement found on the Model T and most other cars. The drawback was that top speed was limited with the worm-drive – although, given the state of the roads of rural America in 1918, a high top speed was hardly a priority.

Ford retained a four-cylinder layout when the Model A was introduced in 1927, but power was up sharply. The 200 cu. in. engine produced 40 hp – double that of the Model T – at 2200 rpm. Torque was a respectable 128 ft. lb. This engine made the Model A-based pickup a much more versatile vehicle, with smoother acceleration, higher top speed and greater carrying capacity.

Ford's rivals, however, were moving away from the four-banger in favor of six-cylinder engines, which were smoother-running than a four-cylinder engine of similar size. In 1929 Chevrolet's pickups were avail-

able with an engine that was nicknamed the "Stovebolt Six," a reference to its durability. The name was apt, because although it was continuously updated, the basic design remained in production until 1963. When launched, the Stovebolt Six had 194 cu. in. and produced 50 hp at 2,600 rpm.

Dodge came out with several six-cylinder engines in 1933, replacing its 48 hp four. The base 50 hp six – borrowed from Plymouth, which also built trucks from 1935 to 1942 – was 189 cu. in., and the larger Dodge version, of 201 cu in., produced 70 horsepower at 3,600 rpm.

Even Willys-Overland, a truck maker that would eventually be renamed Willys Jeep, and then just Jeep, had a 65 hp six.

Ultimately, all these six-cylinder engines, used in both trucks and passenger cars, forced Ford to abandon the four-cylinder engine. Working on an unusually tight 18-month deadline, three Ford engineers – Donald Sullivan, Carl Schultz and Ray

Laird – came up with the revolutionary flathead V-8, which debuted in 1932 as an option in Ford automobiles. The flathead was ground-breaking because until then a V-8 had been considered too exotic for mass production because of problems in casting an iron V-shaped block. Ford solved that problem, producing a 221 cu. in. engine that produced 65 hp at 3200 rpm. That 65 hp rating was misleading, however. The first V-8s had the very low compression ratio of 5.5 to 1 and a restrictive carburetor. Engine tweakers, who later became known as hot-rodders, quickly saw the engine's potential and it soon became easy for enthusiasts to significantly increase the V-8's output.

The V-8 was first listed as a truck option in late 1932, and was widely available starting with the 1933 models. By 1934 the V-8 was the engine of choice for Ford truck buyers, and in 1935 the four-cylinder engine was dropped from production.

For more than two decades, the flathead Ford V-8 was regarded as the cutting-edge in light-duty pickup engines.

BELOW *This Ford Model A truck was considered quite stylish, with its curved side opening on the cab and the port-hole rear windows.*

GMC: CHEVROLET'S TWIN

Truck buyers today know GMC as the truck-only division of General Motors, and the pickups that come with the GMC label are in almost all regards identical to the pickups that can be found in Chevrolet showrooms.

But whereas pickups, and sport-utility vehicles such as Suburbans and Blazers, are the only trucks produced by Chevrolet, they represent merely the starting point for GMC, which produces a variety of trucks of all sizes, including the big tractors that pull commercial trailers.

GMC (a loose acronym for General Motors Truck and Coach Division) can trace its roots to two pioneer truck companies, Rapid and Reliance. At the time these two companies were gobbled up in 1914 by GM's founder, William Durant, they were both building large, chain-driven trucks. After their acquisition Durant kept them as separate builders for a short while before he merged them into GMC. The first truck to carry the GMC label appeared in 1915, a shaft-drive hauler called Model 15. As was common practice at the time, Model 15 was a bare chassis that the buyer then had fitted with an appropriate body.

Over the years, the light-duty trucks produced by GMC became more closely linked with the Chevrolet

RIGHT *One of the companies that would try to survive against the Big Three after World War II was Willys-Overland, which was famous for its military Jeep. This 1950 truck boasted a more powerful engine lineup called Hurricane. Willys would eventually become known as Jeep and, in the 1980s, be swallowed up by Chrysler.*

trucks as a way of keeping costs down. By the 1930s, there was very little difference between a GMC pickup and a Chevrolet. Today, the GMC S-15 pickup is identical to the Chevrolet S-10. Other twins are the GMC Sierra and Chevrolet C/K full-sized pickup, the GMC Yukon and Chevrolet Blazer, and the Suburban, which carries the same name at both GMC and Chevrolet.

Because of its wider dealer network, Chevrolet outsells GMC by a substantial margin. So why does General Motors build identical GMC and Chevrolet trucks? Primarily it's a marketing decision. While Chevrolet's truck customers are often crossovers from the car line, GMC caters more directly to businesses and fleet customers. The feeling within GM is that it has a marketing advantage in selling to commercial users with a company that devotes all its efforts to one thing – trucks.

That's not to say that the general public doesn't also buy from GMC. Many of the GMC truck dealerships are paired with other GM franchises, such as Pontiac, which doesn't offer any trucks. And some truck buyers are more than happy to buy a GMC-badged S-15 simply because it is a slightly rarer model than a Chevy S-10.

DRIVING ALL FOUR WHEELS

The popularity of four-wheel drive in light-duty pickups is a relatively recent phenomenon. Excluding rare, one-off conversions, the first time four-wheel-drive was offered on a mass-produced pickup was in 1936 at Ford.

Late in that model year, Ford contracted with an Indianapolis, IN, company called Marmon-Herrington to convert its vehicles – both cars and trucks – to four-wheel drive on a special-order basis. When a customer specified a four-wheel-drive truck (or car), Ford shipped a complete vehicle to Marmon-Herrington, which then proceeded to rebuild much of the drive line and chassis. The body was removed and the chassis lengthened by an inch and a half. Springs were changed and, in early conversions, the stock cable-operated brakes were replaced by a hydraulic setup. The front-drive axle was a standard Ford rear-drive axle fitted with steering knuckles. The ratio on both axles was 4.44:1 and they were engaged by a single-range transfer case located behind the four-speed manual transmission. Because of the low demand for four-wheel-drive vehicles,

Ford farmed out the conversions to Marmon-Herrington until 1959, when it began to build them in Ford's own factories.

Chevrolet followed a path similar to Ford's, but not until 1947. The Chevy conversions were done by a Minneapolis, MN, company called Napco. The option was called Mountain Goat, now very rare.

Willys-Overland, the company that gets credit for building the four-wheel-drive World War II jeep, began to offer four-wheel drive vehicles produced at its own factory in 1946. What's not widely known, however, is that it was Marmon-Herrington Fords that the U.S. Army used as the prototype for the jeep that Willys and others built during the war.

Dodge also took advantage of what it learned during wartime and in 1946 began offering a line called Power Wagons. These were incredibly brawny, high-riding trucks that made few concessions to passenger comfort. Although only about 3,000 were sold that first year, the Power Wagon name would carry on at Dodge through 1980.

BELOW The modern pickup design as exemplified by this 1980 Dodge uses smooth sides on the pickup box and a broad, flat grille.

A change in the tastes and needs of American car buyers after World War II would alter the way pickups were designed and marketed. Before the war, the main buyers of pickups were the significant number of Americans who lived on small farms and ranches.

Such things as softer suspensions and in-dash radios were hardly features that farmers wanted on their trucks. So basic were some trucks, such as the standard Dodge model of 1945, that shock absorbers – which were standard on the Dodge sedan – were deleted from the pickup.

Still, pickups and other small trucks were among the first new vehicles to become available to civilians after nearly four years of wartime automotive deprivation, and they were highly sought after. It mattered little that these were military trucks that simply traded one shade of green paint that the Army called olive drab for one that Chevrolet called Brewster Green. In fact, Chevrolet made the advertising pitch that these trucks had been put to the ultimate test and were ultra-rugged:

"To help refill the war-depleted highways of America as soon as possible, Chevrolet presents, with no engineering delay, new lines of time-tested trucks for 1946. Based on the 1941 model vehicles, our last truly prewar trucks and the best-designed trucks Chevrolet has ever manufactured heretofore, the new trucks are improved by the

RIGHT *This 1947 Dodge WC pickup is a carry-over model from the trucks that Dodge built as part of the U.S. war effort. Although it looks like a panel delivery model, it really is a pickup with a canvas covering for the bed.*

experience gained in five years of developing military trucks, five years of intense research in materials, five years of study of Chevrolet trucks on the largest proving ground in the world ... the highways of America ... in the particularly tough job of war transportation."

But offering repainted war trucks would not carry the market for long. After World War II, returning soldiers went to college under the G.I. Bill and set their sights on a more sophisticated urban lifestyle. Home-building boomed as more and more people gave up the rural life for cities and the newly emerging suburbs. Pickups gradually came to be a part of that lifestyle, both as utility vehicles for businesses and as weekend carry-alls for homeowners, who were bent on putting up picket fences around their half-acre of the American dream. Although still very much a work horse, the pickup began to take on some sophistication.

Ford touted the "living room comfort" of the cabs on its new lines of F-Series pickups that debuted in 1948. While utilitarian features, such as room for three adult men on the bench seat and a minimum half-ton cargo capacity, were paramount, the F-1

designers put in such features as an adjustable driver's seat with coil springs. In 1947, Chevrolet came out with a new design that emphasized greater visibility from the cab, as well as modern styling cues. It was still utilitarian, however. In typical standard form it had only one tail light and no turn signals. A second tail light and directional signals could be added as extra-cost options.

Nonetheless, the pickups that started appearing in 1946 were significant in that they began to be engineered and marketed in a manner more befitting a passenger car. Detroit was paying attention to what the buyer wanted.

The Advance Design truck series that Chevrolet unveiled in May, 1947 was the most striking of the new trucks, boasting more than 30 new features. The Advance Design trucks had passenger cabs that offered better visibility, more comfortable seating, column-mounted gear selector, easier door access and a better ride. The trucks were available with standard and Deluxe cabs. The Deluxe cab pickups were notable for their wraparound glass rear-quarter windows, which replaced the standard metal panel on

ABOVE *By the 1949 model year, Chevrolet trucks had established themselves as a sales leader. Restyled in 1947, these trucks were called Advance Design models.*

the base pickup. The Deluxe cab models were also known as "five-window" trucks: two-pane front windshield, two curved rear-quarter glass panels, and flat rear-window pane. With all that glass, the Deluxe cab trucks gave the driver and passenger an unprecedented all-round view.

The new trucks were an instant success, and by 1950 Chevrolet accounted for one-third of all U.S. truck sales, with production that year setting a record at more than 494,000 vehicles. The Advance Design pickups would remain in production for seven years virtually unchanged – side-vent windows in '51, push-button door handles in '52, a new windshield and automatic transmission in '53.

Ford, Dodge and the other pickup manufacturers were not caught flat-footed by the Advance Design models, but they largely had to fight for second place in sales behind Chevrolet. Ford, invigorated by a "brain trust" of executives hired after the war to revamp the company that Henry Ford founded and had left to his heirs when he died on April 7, 1947, at age 83, brought a new line of trucks to market in

early 1948. Called the F-Series, these trucks also were designed to cater to buyers who were becoming as style conscious as the car buyers.

The F-Series pickups had cabs that had more room and were more comfortable than any previous Ford truck. The new cab was taller, wider and longer, and the chassis was redesigned to cushion passengers better from bumps and road noise. The instrument panel was all-new, featuring a speedometer with odometer, and engine temperature, oil pressure, battery charging and fuel gauges. An option was a push-button radio. Power came from the standard 226 cu. in. six-cylinder engine or an optional 100 hp 239 cu. in. V-8. A sales pitch that Ford used on these trucks was that they were "Bonus Built" – implying that they came with more features as standard than the competition. While Ford sales were strong, they lagged behind Chevrolet.

Dodge brought its post-war truck design to market in 1948, and, like Chevrolet and Ford, the theme of the new pickups was more comfort and style than had ever been seen before in a truck.

BELOW *The Advance Design Chevrolet pickups boasted more than 30 new features, including a softer ride. This Deluxe cab model has wraparound rear quarter windows.*

LEFT *Dodge called its post-war truck design the Pilot House Safety Cab, which was a reference to greatly improved visibility due to increases in windshield and side glass area.*

Called the PIlot House Safety Cab, the new Dodge featured a cockpit that was higher, wider, longer and better insulated than previous models. To reduce vibration and road noise, the cab was mounted on four rubber mounts, and a solid, one-piece floorboard was installed. The seat was mounted on rollers so that it could be adjusted fore and aft to suit a variety of drivers. The seat height was increased to improve overall visibility.

Like Chevrolet, Dodge offered a Deluxe cab that included rear-quarter windows, though the Dodge design was not in the wrap-around style of the Chevy model. But for pickup buyers who really wanted luxury, Dodge offered a Custom model that came standard with more comfortable seat and back cushions, sun visors, an arm rest on the driver's door, and electric (as opposed to the old style vacuum-powered) windshield wipers. While all these changes may seem trivial in our era of trucks with compact-disc stereos and leather captain's chairs, for truck buyers after World War II they were unheard of treats that were quickly gobbled up.

With all this truck consumption going on, it was natural to assume that the key players in the market before World War II would become even stronger after the war. But the market was harsh to those who were not quick to react to change. Such names as Willys/Jeep, International and Studebaker would simply be outgunned in production, engineering and marketing resources by the giants of the light-truck field – Ford, Chevrolet/GMC and Dodge.

What happened to International immediately after World War II is a good example. While Ford, Chevrolet and Dodge had their restyled, modern trucks in showrooms in 1947 and '48, it took smaller International until 1950 to come out with its L-Series pickups. Although arguably an able competitor, the L-Series had an impossible fight to win buyers over from the Big Three.

Studebaker lagged even farther behind in the race for truck sales, and Willys survived not on its truck sales, but on its trusty Jeep and other four-wheel-drive specialty vehicles. Studebaker closed up shop for good in 1964, and Willys went through a series of

ABOVE *By the early 1950s, the Dodge pickup design showed some modern themes, such as a lower profile for the cab and opening side vent windows. This Deluxe cab model has three rear windows, similar to the Chevrolet design.*

27

ABOVE *International was one of the fading pickup truck competitors in the 1950s. Although this 1958 model has a number of modern features and attractive styling, it couldn't compete with the Fords and Chevys.*

corporate restructurings and takeovers before becoming a part of Chrysler in the late 1980s.

International certainly proved the most game competitor, keeping its pickup line until 1975, when the company abandoned full-sized light-duty trucks to concentrate its resources in its heavy-duty commercial truck division.

So for most Americans, the choice in pickups during the incredible economic boom of the 1950s was Ford, Chevrolet (and its clone GMC) or Dodge, and those three fought hard for buyers, bringing out new trucks that offered more and more features that went beyond basic hauling.

In an effort to take a bit out of Chevrolet's phenomenal success with its Advance Design trucks, Ford in 1953 – the company's Golden Anniversary year – brought out its F-100 lineup, which significantly upped the ante. Many collectors argue that the F-100 is the best-looking truck of its era, and today it is among the most collectable.

The F-100 had modern, rounded corners, a big, wide, aggressive grille and a one-piece slanted and curved windshield that gave the cab a more aerodynamic look. The pickup box was longer at 6½ feet and had a 20-inch depth that gave it more cargo capacity than the basic Chevy and Dodge trucks.

The F-100 was a pacesetter in the growing trend toward trucks that offered more car-like comforts. The cab was wider and, thanks to the curved windshield, offered an even better view of the road. The doors were longer and had wider openings. The bench seat was wide enough for three adult men and had "no-sag" springs. The instrument panel was curved, similar to the setup in the passenger cars, which had been redesigned the year before. On Deluxe cab models, buyers also received more sound-deadening material to insulate the cab, a padded headliner, and door locks. Two-tone upholstery was also available on Deluxe Cab models.

A shorter wheelbase (110 in) and a redesigned front suspension also helped make the F-100 an easier vehicle to maneuver in city traffic, an environment in which more and more pickup trucks were being used. One of the big selling points on the new model was that all the features combined to reduce driver fatigue, thereby making it a safer vehicle.

The most ground-breaking new feature on the Ford, however, was the optional Fordomatic automatic transmission. Eliminating the need to shift gears helped further blur the lines between cars and trucks and, as far as marketing went, made the pickup more accessible to women drivers. Although the trend

RIGHT *International gave up the full-size pickup market in the 1970s and concentrated on large commercial trucks. This 1975 Model 150 was one of the last the company made.*

toward automatic transmissions in trucks would not really take off for another 20 years, its introduction in 1953 on the F-100 was visionary.

The final link with the prewar models of Ford trucks was severed in 1954 when the venerable flathead V-8 was dropped in favor of a new overhead valve V-8 that was based on a deep Y-shaped cast-iron block. The new V-8 had the same displacement as the flathead (239 cu. in.) but developed more power (130 hp). Also available in the pickup was a 223 cu. in. six rated at 115 hp.

Dodge was a year behind in replacing its Pilot House Safety Cab design with a model that could compete with the Ford F-100. A distant third in sales to Chevrolet and Ford, Dodge took something of a middle road in building a new pickup. There was more emphasis on creature comforts – a lower cab and lower running-board height for easier entry, and a lower front hood for a better road view – but there was something of a back-to-basics appeal as well.

Dubbed the Functional Design Era, the 1954–6 Dodge trucks were sold on a campaign of rugged utility. The cab was almost devoid of ornamentation, and the body had only a minute amount of chrome – amazing when you consider that this truck debuted in the hey-day of heavily chromed cars. But the cab's window area was increased and the bench seat was fitted with new cushions with more pillowy springs. In an early nod toward driver ergonomics, the glove box was repositioned from the passenger side of the

dashboard to the center, so that the driver could more easily retrieve something from it without having to bend over.

The new Dodge trucks also had some other notable features. An automatic transmission, called the Truck-O-Matic, was an option, as was the first V-8 to appear in a Dodge truck. If you're handing out prizes to the first truck line to feature an automatic gearbox, some 1949 Dodges would be the winner. Those trucks were offered with Fluid Drive, a semi-automatic transmission that had first appeared on Chryslers in 1939. The Fluid Drive truck retained the foot-operated clutch for starting the engine. Once the engine was running and either a high or low range was selected, it was unnecessary to shift again. If the vehicle was brought to a halt, the Fluid Drive would idle with the clutch engaged because the hydraulic system would allow clutch slippage until engine speed increased the pressure and the gearbox became fully engaged. In 1954 the Fluid Drive was renamed the Truck-O-Matic and, although the clutch was retained for engine starts, the transmission operated much more like the clutchless automatics offered by Chevrolet and Ford.

The Dodge V-8 that appeared on June 1, 1954 was a 241 cu. in. overhead-valve design that produced 145 hp, giving Dodge bragging rights to "The World's Most Powerful Pickup." As an advertising gimmick, the truck was taken to the Bonneville Salt Flats for pre-production testing, although no numbers were released on what its top speed might have been. The V-8 was optional and a 230 cu. in. six was standard.

Despite its all-new truck, Dodge sales in 1954 were disastrous, dropping from a peak a few years earlier of nearly 200,000 to just 104,966. The nose-dive was due in part to a slowing in the post-war economy: all truck sales were down in that year. But it also was due to the fierce sales fight going on between Ford and Chevrolet, who were spending millions of dollars to promote their trucks in an effort to claim No. 1 status.

Chevrolet held the lead in sales despite Ford's best efforts and the fact that Chevy had stuck with the Advance Design pickups it had introduced in 1947. Those trucks proved they had staying power with buyers, despite styling that had become stodgy and the lack of V-8 power.

The bad news for the competition was that in 1955 Chevrolet introduced a new line of trucks that were so stunning they were to influence truck design for the next 40 years. Called the Task Force Series, these trucks came at a time when General Motors was a worldwide power and could seemingly do no wrong.

Styled by the same Harley Earl-led GM team that produced the 1953 Corvette, the 1955 pickups – particularly the sleek Cameo Carrier – were a significant break with the past. Gone were running boards and very upright cabs. These trucks took the slightly rounded theme that Ford and Dodge played with – and took it several steps forward. The egg-crate grille design of the Task Force Chevys was distinctive and made a link to the passenger care lineup, which also was new for 1955. The bulging rear fenders that protruded from the pickup bed were slimmed down considerably (and in the case of the Cameo Carrier eliminated altogether) and the running board was replaced with a built-in step just to the rear of the cab doors.

Inside the cab there was a curved dashboard that had a cowl lip over the instrument panel, which was housed in a V-shaped pod. The cowl lip reduced glare on the instruments, which was a good thing because the truck's wrap-around windshield greatly increased incoming light and outward field of vision. Seat cushions – made from a plastic-rayon woven fabric – and matching embossed, painted metal door panels

BELOW When Dodge added a V-8 to its pickup line in 1954, it boasted that its trucks were the most powerful on the road. The 241 cu. in. V-8 produced 145 horsepower.

were new, and in upgraded models the seat cushions were foam-padded.

The new trucks were more than pretty faces. For the first time Chevrolet offered a V-8 in its pickup trucks. The 265 cu. in. V-8 produced 162 hp, and was of such an advanced design that today's 5.7-liter Chevrolet engine is a direct descendant. The new engine was exactly what the hot-rodders had been waiting for, and it would help the Chevy truck overtake the Ford as a favorite of performance enthusiasts. In one swoop, Chevy shed its image as a maker of dowdy but dependable trucks.

Also technically significant, if less talked about, was the debut of an open driveshaft differential on the pickup – something Chevy's competitors were switching to as well. Previously the engine had transmitted its power to the rear axle using what was called a torque tube. Although workable, the torque tube wasn't as sturdy in high-horsepower applications. What an open drive shaft allowed Chevrolet to do was to add an electric overdrive unit to the drive line. Overdrive-equipped pickups could cruise comfortably all day at 70 mph without running the engine at full-throttle. As more high-speed highways began to spread across America, such easy cruising became important to pickup buyers.

As the 1960s began, the move was in full swing to make pickups ever more modern and stylish. And as pickups began to exhibit styling statements of their own, so the design link between passenger cars and trucks was at last severed. (The exceptions, of course, were the El Camino and Ranchero).

As a concession to style, Ford made a radical change in how it constructed its pickups, starting in 1961 – a change it would regret. Traditionally, pickups are built as two boxes – the front cab and the rear cargo bed – anchored to a separate frame. This worked fine, but it has two drawbacks: there is wasted space between where the cargo bed ends and the cab begins; and there is always this ugly gap that runs vertically down the middle of the vehicle.

On Ford trucks built between 1961 and 1964, the cab and the cargo bed were one unit, creating a stronger vehicle when it came to chassis flex and providing a smoother-looking design when looked at from the side. The problem came when the cargo bed began to rust – as it certainly did, given the then limited technology in corrosion prevention and the abuse to which pickups are routinely subjected. On conventional trucks, a pickup owner could just unbolt the rusted cargo bed, throw it away, and put on a new one. On the one-piece Fords, that was not an option.

So irate were Ford buyers that, in 1965, Ford quietly brought back the two-box construction of its trucks. Things were better at Chevrolet, which continued to dominate the U.S. truck market. The basic design introduced in 1955 continued into the 1960s with minor styling updates that stressed function over form.

In 1963 Chevrolet made two important changes under the skin of its pickup. The long-standing torsion-bar suspension was discarded in favor of a cheap-to-manufacture coil-spring front suspension that also gave the pickup a more carlike ride. And the venerable Stovebolt Six engine, which had been in service from 1929 to 1962, was gone, in favor of a new 230 cu. in. in-line six that shared many design features with the Chevy small-block V-8. The new six produced 140 hp in its base configuration.

Ford's big news in 1965 was the introduction of its twin I-beam front suspension, a setup that was rugged and, according to Ford ads, gave its trucks greater ability to handle rough roads and tough hauling. It proved to be a popular design: the I-beam suspension remained on every full-sized Ford truck until the 1997 model.

How big had trucks become by the mid 1960s? When Chevrolet began building trucks in 1918, it sold one truck for every 102 of its cars. By the 1960s that ratio had dropped to one truck for every six cars. Even Dodge, the perennial third-place finisher in the truck sales race, benefited from the popularity of trucks in general. Its sales skid stopped in 1961, and an upturn in 1962 – thanks mostly to better marketing and the introduction of a small van – pushed sales over the 100,000 mark. In the mid 1960s Dodge adopted a policy of not introducing a new model year truck in the fall – a Detroit marketing tradition for decades. Rather, Dodge would simply bring a new model to market whenever it was ready. For example, a heavily revised D100 pickup was introduced in the spring of 1965, without much fanfare. Nonetheless, Dodge sales continued to climb as the overall demand for pickups continued strong, boosted by a red-hot economy and two-vehicle families in which the second car was more and more often a truck.

Of more serious concern to Dodge was that it was losing market share to Ford and Chevrolet. True, Dodge was selling more cars – but not nearly as many as its two main competitors. When the 1970s rolled around, Ford and Chevrolet were selling more than 700,000 trucks of all types each year, whereas Dodge built about 175,000 in a good model year.

BELOW This 1964 Dodge D100 pickup was the standard hauler from Chrysler. It featured the venerable slant-six engine and a 6½-foot cargo bed.

RIGHT *Starting in the
1970s, pickups came in all
manner of sizes and styles. The
SuperCab pickup that Ford
introduced in 1974 (top) had
extended interior room and
made pickups more attractive to
families. Using the family
pickup for camping was
becoming more common, and
this prototype bed-mounted tent
was one effort to capitalize on
the trend. Some people wanted
the versatility of a pickup but in
a smaller size. The Japanese
manufacturers started to exploit
that niche, so The Big Three
countered by buying pickups in
Japan and putting their name on
them. This 1973 Ford Courier
started life as a Mazda. High-
performance pickups have been
offered on a limited-edition basis
for years. The 1978 Dodge
Adventurer was nicknamed Lil
Red Express Truck, and came
from the factory with chrome
wheels and dual exhausts that
rose skyward just behind the cab.
For the more utilitarian buyer,
Dodge also offered a factory-
built tow truck option for the
1974 D300 Club Cab. And
for buyers who really wanted to
haul, there were trucks such as
the 1978 Chevrolet Crew Cab
Dooley, which had four doors
and dual rear wheels for
maximum payload.*

Throughout the 1960s and into the 1970s, Ford and Chevrolet continued to counter each other with new designs and expensive marketing campaigns to make sure they were the sales leaders. The result was that the truck market became more sophisticated, more a twin of the automobile market that had existed since World War II.

What was happening in the 1970s was that the pickup market was splintering into distinct types of trucks to meet specialized needs: plain Jane work trucks; pickups designed to carry camper units in the cargo bed (a segment that Dodge exploited heavily); pickups with extended cabs that allowed the owner to carry an extra passenger behind the front bench seat; pickups with dual rear wheels ("doolies") that could tow 10,000 lb trailers; four-door pickups; pickups with bulging rear fenders; pickups with smooth sides; compact pickups with gas-sipping four-cylinder engines; pickups with fire-breathing V-8s; and pickups with bucket seats, air-conditioning, power windows and AM-FM stereo radios. Whatever a buyer wanted in a pickup, the market provided.

The popularity of pickups in the 1970s was boosted by an unlikely player: the federal government. Starting in 1970, severe emission restrictions were being placed on passenger cars by federal enactments. These came after several years of safety mandates, and they were followed in 1973 by the Arab oil embargo, which prompted the government to step in and order economy standards.

The sum of these actions, in the eyes of many consumers, was to make cars less fun to drive. Power was down, costs were up to cover the new federal mandates, and the vehicles themselves were becoming ever more complicated for the average backyard mechanic to work on. Most pickups, however, were immune to these changes in character, in large part because the federal government was slower to apply safety, emission and fuel economy standards to vehicles the bureaucrats saw as largely commercial. The equation for pickups was that they were four-wheeled vehicles with powerful engines that had an almost charming utilitarian character. And in many cases in the 1970s they were thousands of dollars cheaper than their passenger-car cousins.

So pickups as recreational or leisure vehicles became a cult happening. Teenagers who 10 years

LEFT *So how tough are pickups? This 1960 Ford F350 is still seeing duty in Colombia, although its pickup bed has long since been replaced.*

earlier might have bought a Pontiac GTO, instead bought a Ford F-150 Ranger XLT Styleside with a 390 cu. in. V-8, four-speed manual transmission, loud exhaust and chrome wheels. Two-car families found that an extended-cab pickup made sense as a weekend vehicle that could be used for garage sales.

By the time the 1970s closed and the 1980s (known to some as the me-decade) opened, the pickup, in all its permutations, was well situated to become the status vehicle of American life.

WHAT'S IN A NAME?

U.S. pickup truck builders have over the decades developed model designations that serve to indicate the cargo capacities of their full-sized vehicles, as measured in fractions of a ton (2,000 pounds).

Ford started the trend in 1948 with the F-series pickups. The F-1, which was the basic pickup, was rated at a half-ton cargo capacity, the minimum load that qualifies a vehicle as a full-sized pickup. The F-2 was rated at three-quarters of a ton, and the F-3 was listed as a one-ton hauler. In 1953, the numbers changed slightly. The new F-100 was the half-ton model, the F-250 could take three quarters of a ton and the F-350 was rated at a full ton. When the F-150 debuted in 1975, it became the half-ton designation, while the F-250 and F-350 kept their ratings.

Chevrolet was a bit slower to standardize model numbers in relation to cargo capacity. In the 1950s

Chevy pickups rated for a half-ton were called the 3100 Series, with the 3200 Series being rated for three-quarters of a ton, and a one-ton pickup either being a 3600 Series or a 3800 Series, depending on its designation as a double-duty truck or a heavier commercial pickup. In the 1960s the numbers were simplified to Series 10 (half ton), Series 20 (three quarter ton), and Series 30 (one ton). In 1987, the numbers changed to 1500 (half ton), 2500 (three quarter ton) and 3500 (one ton). Also, the addition of the letter C to a model number denoted a two-wheel-drive truck, the letter K a four-wheel-drive.

ABOVE *Among the most attractive pickups from the 1950s, this 1957 Chevrolet was a durable hauler. This model is a bare-bones example, with a painted front bumper and grille, and very little chrome. The spotlight and the white wall tires were optional.*

In 1957, Dodge adopted a numerical system that saw the half-ton pickup numbered D100, the three quarter ton D200 and the one ton D300.

To further confuse matters, in almost every case these ratings on today's trucks understate the actual carrying capacity of the vehicle. For example, Chevrolet's half-ton standard pickup is rated by the factory as being safely able to carry 1,500 lb, or three-quarters of a ton! Although no one at Ford,

Chevy or Chrysler can explain exactly how this all came about, it's generally accepted that the first trucks to be rated as half-ton models could carry no more than that, but that, as the capacity grew over the years, the convenient numbering system remained unchanged as a way of indicating the relationship between the cargo capacity of a different models of the same make, as opposed to an accurate statement of the maximum weight each could carry.

BELOW *This 1957 Dodge D100 pickup has single front headlamps set in deep fairings, a chrome front bumper, and runnings boards.*

CHEVROLET'S CAMEO CARRIER: AHEAD OF ITS TIME

In spite of all the creature comforts that Chevrolet, Ford and Dodge engineered into their pickups, until 1955, it's unarguable that pickup trucks were built with one primary purpose in mind: work. Their car-like front cabs were crafted onto bulky pickup beds that were designed to take a lot of abuse, because that's what they got from buyers.

Chevrolet broke that mold in 1955 when it introduced the Cameo Carrier, a pickup that was conceived from the start to be as glamorous as any sports car. Styled by a young GM designer named Chuck Jordan, who would eventually rise to be chief corporate designer from the 1970s through the early 1990s, the Cameo Carrier had flush-sided exterior panels that gave the overall truck a streamlined appearance. Chrome bumpers, body side trim and tail lights combined with white-wall tires and wheel covers from the passenger car line gave the Cameo Carrier a show-truck quality. The special red-and-beige upholstery, red floor mats, red-rimmed steering wheel and red-painted cargo box liner on the debut 1955 model helped that image along.

Perhaps the most sought after collectable pickup from the 1950s, the Cameo Carrier was in many regards a smoke-and-mirrors creation. In reality it was a Deluxe Stepside pickup with fiberglass add-on cargo-box fenders that covered the wheel fenders on the normal truck. These fenders gave the truck the appearance of having a custom wide-cargo bed, but it was in fact the same as a stock pickup. And all those trim items that looked like they were off a

ABOVE When Ford introduced its 1970 Ranger pickup, an added trim level called the XLT was offered. The XLT model offered special chrome trim on the outside, as well as a long list of car-like amenities on the inside.

contemporary Chevrolet passenger car were unique to the Cameo Carrier, which also carried a separate model number from all other pickups. The only interchangeable car/truck items were the wheel covers. A truck item that was unique to the Cameo Carrier was a seven-piece fiberglass rear bumper assembly that had a hinged cover where the spare tire was concealed underneath the cargo bed.

GMC wasn't left out of the glamour truck field. The Cameo Carrier was renamed a Suburban pickup when it was sold through GMC dealers. The primary differences were changes to the grille and the use of a Pontiac V-8 as an option.

In terms of total sales in its lifespan of a little more than three years, the Cameo Carrier was merely a blip on the sales chart. From 1955 through early 1958, when the Cameo Carrier was dropped, Chevrolet sold more than 1 million trucks. Cameo Carrier sales for that same period were considerably less than 5,000.

But where the Cameo Carrier had a big impact was in pointing the way toward the future of the pick-

up. Here was a truck that had the sort of style that would not embarrass its owner when he drove it to the country club. Yet it had enough cargo capacity for light hauling jobs on the work site or at weekends. The styling theme of the Cameo Carrier – the flat-sided cargo box – would be adopted for the more mainstream 1958 Chevrolet Apache pickup and would influence truck design for decades.

THE DRIVE FOR 4X4s

It's incongruous that the popularity of pickups with four-wheel drive has risen so dramatically in spite of the millions of miles of paved road available in the United States. In the early days of the pickup, when America was just starting construction of its vast highway network, there would have been a real need for four-wheel-drive pickups. But it wasn't until just before World War II that a workable, compact all-wheel-drive system was made available. Credit for the first factory-authorized four-wheel-drive option must go to Ford, which, as we have seen, contracted as early as 1936 with the Marmon-Herrington company to take two-wheel-drive trucks and convert them to four-wheel-drive by adding a front differential and transfer case.

The first factory-built four-wheel-drive pickup, the Power Wagon, was offered in 1946 by Dodge, and a year later Willys-Overland introduced its Jeep four-wheel-drive pickup. Both these trucks were based on rugged four-wheel-drive vehicles that the companies had built for military use during World War II. To accommodate the extra drive shaft running to the front axe, they had heavy-duty springs that raised the truck's ground clearance to the point that it was a chore climbing into the cab. And the on-road ride was abysmally bumpy. Buyers were primarily limited to industrial and ranch customers. In 1947, for example, only about 4,000 four-wheel-drive Willys trucks of all sorts were sold.

Ford and Chevrolet didn't begin building their own four-wheel-drive pickups until the 1950s. Chevrolet's first factory-built four-wheel-drive pickup appeared in 1957, and Ford's model debuted in 1959. Like the Dodge and Jeep pickups, Chevy and Ford's four-wheel-drive trucks were envisioned as appealing only to people who needed to operate in very rough terrain, such as in logging or mining operations. Therefore there were few amenities, and high ground clearance was considered far more important than ride comfort.

But as Americans began to acquire more leisure time and to take more vacations to off-the-beaten-path places, a change came over the four-wheel-drive

market. Camper bodies mounted onto pickup truck beds began to appear, and folks who wanted to experience the outdoors and take a few comforts along demanded four-wheel-drive, for its ability to plow through snow and mud.

Mirroring the rise in overall pickup popularity, the four-wheel-drive segment of the market began to evolve from rough, non-nonsense trucks into vehicles that offered a compromise between off-road versatility and paved-road manners. Starting in about 1960 and continuing through today, 4 x 4 pickups – as the genre is now known – have seen advances such as low- and high-gear transfer cases that allow all four wheels to be used at any speed, self-locking front hubs, and electric, shift-on-demand systems that allow a drive to choose two-, or four-wheel drive at a moment's notice.

Ride heights have been lowered – in some cases to the point where really rugged off-road use isn't practical – and suspensions have been smoothed to the point where a freeway jaunt no longer shakes a passenger's fillings loose.

Today, having a truck capable of four-wheel-drive operation has become a status symbol – much like having a huge engine in a sports car. Gaudy decals that proclaim a pickup as a 4 x 4 are common marketing insignias slapped on at the factory. In some years, 4 x 4 pickups account for as much as 30 percent of all pickups sold, though it's doubtful if a majority of these 4 x 4s ever see much slogging up a mountain hillside.

LEFT *Although four-wheel-drive pickups are hot items today, they were rarities until the late 1950s. This 1955 Willys was one of the few factory-built four-wheel-drives available.*

El Camino &

There's an old story about how a group of blind men is led to an elephant and, when they are stationed at different points around the animal, each is asked to describe the beast. Needless to say, none of the blind men comes up with a life-like description.

In 1957 at Ford and in 1959 at Chevrolet two vehicles were introduced that were somewhat difficult to classify. Called the Ranchero and the El Camino, these vehicles could be called cars with pickup beds, or trucks with automobile front ends. When the first pickups appeared, they were often cars with pickup beds crudely grafted onto a coupé. The Ranchero and El Camino, however, were only loosely based on that concept.

When Ford introduced the Ranchero, advertising stressed the car's dual nature: it could haul some bulky things, but it was also suitable for comfortable passenger-car use. Ads claimed that the Ranchero shared the two-seat Thunderbird's heritage, but had the versatility of a pickup.

Based on the Fairlane station wagon, the Ranchero was much more of a car than a truck. At a time when all Ford trucks had straight front axles, the Ranchero had a ball joint/coil spring front suspension off the Fairlane. The Ranchero was also the first light-

BELOW One of the first true marriages of a car and a pickup was this 1959 Chevrolet El Camino. Based on the Chevrolet Bel Air coupe, the El Camino was brought out to compete with the Ford Ranchero, which debuted in 1957.

BELOW Dodge tried to compete with the Ranchero and El Camino with its Sweptside D100. While the Ranchero and El Camino were based on a car chassis, the Sweptside was a rebodied truck. It didn't fare well in dealer showrooms and was soon dropped.

duty truck to offer air-conditioning as a factory option, which paired nicely with other available features such as power steering, power brakes, power windows and power seats.

Under the hood Ford offered a wide range of engines, from a 223 cu. in. six to 312 cu. in. V-8s with two four-barrel carburetors, as well as a three-speed automatic transmission. Equipped with the big V-8, a Ranchero could be developed to become a competitor at the nation's emerging drag strips. Yet this same speedster could also be used to haul up to 1,190 lb of cargo in its bed, which was 72 in long. The width of the tailgate made loading and hauling truly bulky items somewhat problematic, however. Where most Rancheros saw duty was as short-trip haulers for gas stations and body shops, as well as on small ranches.

Ranchero:

Pickups masquerading as cars

BELOW *Ford advertised that its Ranchero was a blend of the Thunderbird spirit and pickup versatility. This 1958 model was typical of how these cars were equipped, and most buyers only used them for the lightest of hauling duties.*

ABOVE *Quad square headlamps, a 302 cu. in. V-8 and a fancy racing stripe set the 1977 Ranchero apart from its plainer cousins. By the late 1970s, standard pickups were becoming more stylish and more comfortable, making the Ranchero redundant.*

In 1959, Chevrolet fired back with its El Camino, which looked very similar to that year's Bel Air, a model noted for its flamboyant rear fins, which came at the peak of America's love affair with the Buck Rogers school of design. Like the Ranchero, the El Camino combined all the options available on a car with a pickup truck bed. In the case of the El Camino, the bed also suffered some width restrictions (it was less than four-feet wide) that placed its use as a serious hauler somewhat in doubt. Nonetheless, the long list of options, particularly in the engine compartment, made it a favorite with younger buyers who needed a workhorse but didn't want to give up style.

Dodge countered with a very limited production truck called the Sweptside, which was a pickup customized with the fins popular on the Dodge, Plymouth and Chrysler cars. Not heavily promoted, the Sweptside debuted in 1957 and disappeared in

1959, and Dodge never again made a stab at producing a competitor to the El Camino and Ranchero.

Perhaps because Ford was first to market the concept, or perhaps because buyers were turning off to the whole notion of vehicles with huge fins, the El Camino in the beginning didn't fare as well as the Ranchero. Sales were so slow that Chevrolet withdrew the El Camino after the 1960 model year and didn't introduce the concept again until 1964, when a new El Camino, based on the mid-sized Chevelle, appeared.

During Chevrolet's absence, Ford downsized the Ranchero in 1960 and based it on the new Falcon line. Chevrolet offered its competing Corvair in a pickup version, but its rear-engine design limited its appeal. The Falcon Ranchero had an even smaller payload capacity (800 lb) than the full-sized version it replaced, making it the first true compact pickup offered by a major American company.

Despite its limited carrying capacity, the Falcon Ranchero continued to be popular with people who wanted an attractive little truck that truly drove and looked like a car. In 1966, Ford again moved the Ranchero onto the larger Fairlane chassis, where it remained until 1971. In 1972, it was based on the Gran Torino/LTD II body, which was the Fairlane's replacement. The last of the Rancheros was built in 1979, pushed out to pasture by the increasing popularity of compact pickups.

Chevrolet's El Camino followed a similar road. It was based on the mid-sized Chevelle chassis from 1964 through 1976 – years that many consider to be the model's high water mark. In 1977 the Chevelle series was dropped and a new mid-sized car, called

the Malibu – once a model of Chevelle – was introduced, and the El Camino continued on that chassis until 1987, when the El Camino line was dropped by Chevrolet. In 1971, GMC offered a clone of the El Camino called the Sprint. When the Malibu series was introduced, GMC changed its clone's name to Caballero, and it too continued until 1987.

Most popular among collectors of El Caminos and Rancheros are the high-performance models of the late 1960s and early 1970s. On the Ford side, the most coveted is the 1970 428 cu. in. Cobra Jet V-8 Ranchero, which was as fast as any muscle car in its day. For El Camino fans, the 1970 Super Sport model with the 454 cu. in. V-8 is the ultimate ride. That few of these cars ever saw duty as pickup trucks mattered little. They looked good and could really burn rubber.

BELOW *Although still able to haul heavy loads stylishly, the El Camino was dropped after 1986 because of shifting consumer tastes.*

MINI PICKUPS

While the pickup truck market was rolling strongly through the 1950s and 1960s, a new segment of the market began to emerge: the compact pickup. The diminutive Crosley, which debuted in 1940 and was built on and off until 1962, can claim to be the first compact pickup. But it was never a success, and probably no more than 2,000 were sold in its lifetime.

The start of the modern compact pickup market probably can be pegged to the late 1950s, when two Japanese companies – Toyota and Datsun (now

Nissan) began exporting their small pickups to California. Economical to run and inexpensive to buy, these trucks began to see duty as urban delivery vehicles and around-the-farm work trucks. Although they were crude by today's standards, they were forerunners of what by the 1980s would become a deluge of high-quality Japanese-made cars and trucks on the American market.

A limited dealer network, combined with the fact that, at a time when gasoline sold for 25 cents a gallon, operating a larger truck was not much more expensive, kept most of these Toyotas and Datsuns in California. Nonetheless, Detroit also was dabbling in the small truck market by 1960.

As we saw, Ford downsized its Ranchero into the Falcon lineup – the Dearborn, MI, company's first foray into building compact cars. Chevrolet took the more radical approach of offering the rear-engined Corvair in a pickup configuration notable for its optional side-mounted loading door. In terms of sales, the Falcon Ranchero was more successful than the Corvair Model 95 truck, but neither vehicle found much favor with buyers. By 1965, the Falcon had grown back into the larger Fairlane lineup, and the Corvair pickup had become history.

Meanwhile, the Japanese trucks were becoming better, more reliable and more economical vehicles and were spreading out from California. Content with selling about two million trucks a year, Ford, Dodge and Chevrolet unwisely ignored the growing influence of the Japanese trucks. By the 1970s, the public appetite for Japanese compact pickups – at first generally defined as having less than a half-ton carrying capacity, a six-foot or shorter cargo bed and an overall size about half that of a Ford or a Chevy standard pickup – could no longer be ignored, as U.S. sales shot above six figures.

But Detroit was hampered in its ability to respond to the sales threat. Money available for new-product development was being spent to make passenger cars comply with new federal safety and clean-air regulations, and there simply wasn't the capital to spend on developing an all-new line of trucks. So Chevrolet and Ford made an interesting marketing move that, in the 1980s, they would repeat in some aspects of their passenger car lines: they went to Japan and made deals to import small trucks and put their own name on them. Ford went to Mazda and bought a truck it introduced to buyers as the Courier. Chevrolet went to Isuzu and came back with a truck it called LUV – an acronym for Light Utility Vehicle. Dodge, beset by poor management and tight finances, was late to the game and waited until 1979 to go to Mitsubishi to obtain a small pickup that it called the Dodge D50. It proved to be a good stopgap measure that continued to be a serviceable arrangement well into the 1980s, when both Ford and Chevrolet finally produced their own compact pickups, the Ranger and the S-10.

ABOVE *Mini pickups proved popular with younger buyers, so Dodge spiffed up this D50 with white spoke wheels and a laser-like color bar on the lower side of the body.*

OPPOSITE *Chevrolet's entry in the mini pickup market came from Isuzu in 1972 and was called LUV, an acronym for Light Utility Vehicle.*

chapter 3

Chevrolet

By 1980, Chevrolet found itself in a frustrating position. After decades of being the No. 1 producer of light-duty trucks in the United States, it had lost the top pickup truck position to arch rival Ford in the late 1970s and was struggling to regain that title.

What particularly hampered Chevrolet — and all other automobile manufacturers in the early 1980s — was a very weak American economy. The second oil embargo of 1979, combined with stratospheric interest rates, prompted most people to take a wait-and-see attitude toward buying anything that they considered to be a luxury, like a new vehicle. Spending a large amount of money was some risk.

At Chevrolet, that meant its total light-duty truck sales — including vans and sport utility vehicles — dropped below the one million mark for the first time since 1976. Pickups continued to be the most popular trucks, however, accounting for more than half of the 737,788 Chevy trucks built in calendar year 1980.

The start of the 1980s also signaled an historic moment for Chevy trucks. In an acknowledgement of where its future success was likely to be, in mid-1980 Chevrolet discontinued its line of trucks with cargo capacities of more than one ton in order to concentrate on its light-duty models. The sales of heavy-duty Chevy trucks had been dwindling steadily for a number of years, supplanted in large part by those of Chevrolet's sister division, GMC, which produced nothing but trucks.

Although the 1980s started on a down note as far as overall sales were concerned, by 1983 Chevrolet — along with Ford — would begin to enjoy an unprecedented upsurge in pickup sales, thanks to a recovering economy, the expansion of some middle-class families from two-car to three-vehicle households, and a change in the traditional perception that trucks were simply work vehicles.

Although Chevrolet would best Ford's F-series pickup in total sales only in one year — 1982 — and then wind up chasing Ford through 1995 for production dominance, Chevy trucks enjoyed enormous popularity with non-commercial buyers.

Because Chevy trucks employed a standard, car-like ball joint/coil spring/shock absorber front suspension — as opposed to Ford's rugged twin I-beam front suspension — they tended to give a softer ride in everyday use. The Chevy front suspension also lent itself more readily to being lowered, which is a rage among customizers. A further advantage was

the availability of the 350 cu. in. Chevrolet small-block V-8, an engine that can trace its roots back to 1955 and is a darling of the hot-rodders. Aftermarket parts for the Chevy small-block were plentiful and in many cases cheaper than for Ford engines.

So although it is indisputable that during the boom times in the U.S. pickup market, Chevrolet has almost always been behind Ford in sales, Chevy trucks have enjoyed wide popularity and have, over the years, become increasingly refined and car-like in features and handling characteristics.

Here, year-by-year, is a rundown of Chevrolet's pickups since 1980.

1980

Full-sized Chevrolet pickups were available in four trim levels, two body styles and three payload capacities. The basic half-ton Chevy pickup was called the Custom Deluxe, and it was as bare-bones as was possible. There were black vinyl floor mats and there was no upholstered headliner. The front bumper was painted metal, as were the pressed steel wheels and hubcaps. The base engine was a 250 cu. in. straight six that had a two-barrel Rochester carburetor, an 8.3-to-1 compression ratio, and produced 130 hp at 3800 rpm. The basic transmission was a three-speed manual with a column-mounted shift lever. A three-speed Turbo-Hydramatic transmission was optional. Wheelbase was 117.5 inches.

The Custom Deluxe was available with a Fleetside or a Step-Side body. The Fleetside had smooth body panels all the way back from the cab, while the

Step-Side had a contoured rear cargo area with flowing fenders over the rear wheels and a small step integrated into the body just behind the cab doors. Both body styles were available in the three cargo ratings – half-ton, three-quarter-ton and one-ton. The top two rated pickups could also be ordered with Bonus Cab or Crew Cab accommodations. The Bonus Cab had a storage area behind the front bench seat, while the Crew Cab had full front and rear seats. In addition, all three cargo-rated pickups were available in four-wheel-drive configurations.

The option list was long, and began with upgrades in trim, starting with the Scottsdale upgrade, which gave the buyer, among other things, a more comfortable padded bench seat, a cigarette lighter and a chrome front bumper. Next up was the Cheyenne package, which added velour or simulated cowhide vinyl upholstery, sound-deadening material around the cab and the option of bucket seats. Top-of-the-line trim was called the Silverado, which added full gauges, door storage pockets, padded headliner and full carpeting. Other options included air-conditioning, tilt steering wheel, electric clock, Rally wheels and power windows.

In addition to the basic six, other engine options included a 305 cu. in. V-8 rated at 140 hp; a 350 cu. in. V-8 rated at 165 hp; a 400 cu. in. V-8 rated at 185 hp; a 454 cu. in. V-8 rated at 245 hp; and a 350 cu. in. diesel rated at 120 hp.

Because of California's much stricter rules regarding exhaust emissions, not all these engines were available in that state, and those that were may have

ABOVE Although this 1980 Fleetside Silverado is at a job site, more and more trucks by 1980 were being bought for recreational use. The Silverado trim level catered to that market with full carpeting, more comfortable seats, and options such as air-conditioning.

had lower horsepower ratings as a result of power-robbing anti-smog equipment.

1981 The model year started with a re-styled grille and front fenders for the full-sized pickups and the truck-based Blazer and Tahoe. The new front end was slightly more aerodynamic than the previous model and featured a horizontal egg-crate look with four square headlamps when the upper-level trim packages were ordered, or when the optional halogen headlamp feature was ordered on the base pickup.

The interior had a new instrument panel in which the fascia ran the width of the cab and gave the panel a one-piece look. A new trim level called Chevy Sport was offered, which was highlighted with exterior stripes and Sport graphics, as well as a bucket-seat option; and there were the Scottsdale, Cheyenne and Silverado upgrades. Fleetside and Step-Side models continued to be offered.

Overall, Chevrolet put the new pickups on a diet and managed to shave between 80 and 300 lb from their previous weights. Much of the savings came from the use of lighter-weight window glass and lighter steel body panels. Other technical innovations included automatic-locking front wheel hubs on the four-wheel-drive trucks that allowed the driver to shift into all-wheel-drive at speeds of up to 20 mph. Before, four-wheel-drive could be engaged only when the vehicle was stationary.

BELOW For 1981, Chevy pickups such as this Step-Side were put on a diet in the interest of fuel economy and performance. As much as 300 pounds were shaved from some models.

The 1981 model year also marked the first appearance on a Chevy truck of any form of electronic engine controls, a precursor of the fuel-injected, computer-controlled engines of today. Among the engine options in 1981 was a 5-liter V-8 with a four-barrel Rochester carburetor that had electronic spark control. The engine produced 160 hp and 235 foot-pounds of torque. Interestingly, that engine was not available on trucks sold in California because of that state's strict anti-pollution rules. However, electronic spark control was the first step in precisely regulating fuel combustion to ensure cleaner exhaust.

1982 This was the only year Chevrolet bested Ford in the pickup truck sales race since 1976, and much of the credit goes to Chevy's introduction of its S-10 compact pickup, which debuted in mid-1981 as a 1982 model. The appearance of the S-10 was an indication of Chevy's determination to do battle with the Japanese import trucks, but in a market niche of its own making. Bigger than the imported LUV pickup that Chevrolet had been buying from Isuzu and sold with a Chevy badge, the S-10 was significantly smaller than a full-sized pickup.

It was aimed squarely at the recreational or dual-purpose buyer who wanted a pickup but felt the full-sized trucks were too large and not sufficiently economical. The styling was a knockoff of the larger truck, down to the rectangular headlamps and the

A B O V E *This 1981 Fleetside Scottsdale likely saw more time in recreational use than industrial. Note the after-market chrome wheels, the custom pin-striping, and the short 6½-foot cargo bed.*

ABOVE *Although the S-10 was significantly smaller than the half-ton full-size pickup, there were styling similarities, as this rear view of a 1982 Scottsdale Fleetside shows. The model year 1982 was a good one for Chevrolet, allowing it to beat out arch-rival Ford for the No. 1 truck sales title.*

Chevy Bowtie emblem mounted in the center of the front grille. Upgraded Sport and Durango trim options were available.

The S-10 was available in two lengths: a 108 in wheelbase version with a 73.1 in cargo box; and a 122 in wheelbase version with an 89 in box.

Power came from a 1.9-liter, 82 hp four-cylinder engine that was mated to a standard four-speed manual transmission. Optional was a 2.8-liter V-6 that put out 110 hp. At the 1982 Indianapolis 500, a fleet of specially prepared S-10 pickups was used for promotional duties. They had special paint, side-mounted exhaust pipes and Indy 500 logos. More than 177,000 S-10 pickups were sold in 1982 calendar year, compared with about 393,000 full-size pickups.

To cover those buyers who still wanted a mini pickup – and presumably to fulfill its contract with Isuzu – Chevrolet continued offering the LUV pickup in 1982, though it was far outsold by the S-10. The LUV disappeared in 1983 after Chevrolet sold off the last of the 1982 models.

The larger, full-sized pickups continued virtually unchanged, except that the Cheyenne trim and Chevy Sport levels were eliminated, leaving the basic Custom Deluxe, Scottsdale and Silverado models. Four-speed overdrive automatic transmissions were offered as options, in addition to the three-speed automatic gearbox. Four-speed manual transmissions – with or without overdrive – also were offered as options. Engine choices carried over from the previous year, ranging from the standard 250 cu. in. inline six to the 7.4-liter V-8. Step-Side and Fleetside body styles were offered, with the option of a longer 96 in cargo bed on the Fleetside half-ton model.

1983 After its successful launch in 1982, Chevrolet expanded the S-10 line-up with four-wheel-drive and an Extended Cab version that created some stowage space behind the front seat. The S-10 pickup chassis also became the basis of an S-10 Blazer sport-utility vehicle that was a downsized version of the full-size-pickup-based two-door Blazer. Like the pickup, the S-10 Blazer was an instant success. The only other change to the S-10 was the addition of a new 2-liter L-4-design four-cylinder engine that produced 83 hp.

On the full-size truck scene, there was virtually no change from the 1982 models. Advertising copy talked about improved anti-rust protection for the pickup's cargo bed, and there were minor alterations to the front grille and parking lights.

By 1983 the U.S. economy was picking up, and Chevrolet trucks enjoyed a significant improvement in sales over the previous year. S-10 pickup sales were up to 198,000 and full-size pickups topped 412,000. The bad news was that Ford's sales were even higher.

BELOW (TOP) Although dubbed a compact pickup, the S-10 could look quite beefy when equipped with optional four-wheel-drive, alloy wheels and oversized tires. Many S-10 buyers liked the more nimble nature of the S-10 when compared to a full-size truck.

BELOW (BOTTOM) The Extended Cab body style on the full-size pickup was very popular, accounting for nearly a third of all Chevrolet pickup sales. The rear area could be used to haul people for short distances, or store cargo that the owner wanted locked up or protected from the weather.

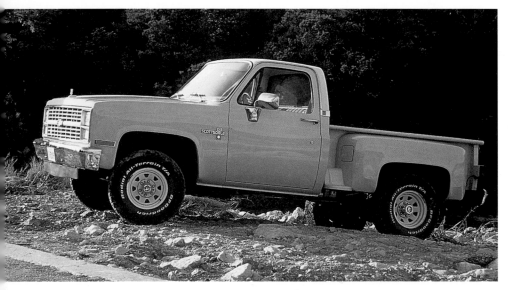

ABOVE (TOP) *Styling on the full-size pickup was virtually unchanged in 1983 from the previous year, and sales continued to climb. More than 412,000 full-size Chevy pickups were sold that year, thanks to a rapidly improving U.S. economy.*

ABOVE (BOTTOM) *The Step-Side body style was not as popular as the Fleetside, but significant numbers of buyers in 1983 liked its retro look and the convenience of the step by the rear wheel fender that made loading or unloading the cargo bed easier.*

1984 The full-size Chevy pickups received a new front grille that incorporated quad square headlamps on all models, as well as a significant list of mechanical and engineering upgrades. Better anti-rust protection for the cab doors was achieved by the use of galvanized steel inner panels, while stone shields for the side-mounted gas tanks and semi-metallic brake linings were among the improvements. Power windows and door locks were offered on the Crew-Cab and Bonus-Cab models.

The 1984 model year saw a proliferation of options, body styles and cargo bed lengths that resulted in Chevy building 39 different types of full-sized pickups. Throw in the two-tone paint schemes that were also offered and it was possible to travel a long way before seeing two identical trucks.

A similar expansion also happened to the S-10, which saw the addition of a Sport model with a special improved-handling suspension. A Tahoe trim package, which offered full carpeting, gauges and other features, was placed over the Durango model. At the top was the Sport model, which added to the Tahoe package a sportier steering wheel and cloth bucket seats with a center floor console. The Extended Cab from the previous year was renamed the Maxi-Cab, and two center-facing jump seats were made options.

1985 For the first time in more than 50 years, no full-size Chevy truck had an in-line six-cylinder engine as standard equipment. New for 1985 was a standard V-6 engine called the Vortec, which Chevrolet claimed to be the most powerful standard engine ever offered in a light-duty pickup. The carbureted Vortec V-6 displaced 4.3-liters and produced 155 hp. Power from traditional Chevy V-8s continued to be available, starting at 5-liters and running up to the 454 cu. in. engine that put out 230 hp.

Styling changes continue to be limited largely to the grille on the pickups, and more two-tone paint schemes.

The big news on the S10 was the deletion of the hyphen from its name and the addition of an S10 badge on the upper portion of the front fenders. A

BELOW Better rust proofing and semi-metallic brake linings were among the improvements made to the full-size pickup line in 1984. This C10 two-wheel-drive model has one of several two-tone paint schemes offered by the factory that year.

LEFT The Silverado trim
package on this 1985 Fleetside
was the top-of-the-line offering,
and buyers could also choose
from a wide-range of engines.
Standard was a 155-horsepower
V-6, replacing the older-
technology in-line six that had
been a Chevy staple for decades.

new 2.5-liter, 92 hp four-cylinder engine with electronic fuel injection was made standard.

Although the overall truck market continued
strong, Chevrolet trucks were starting to lose some
consumer appeal because they had gone so long
without significant changes. A new full-sized truck
was still three years away, so dealers had to make do
with minor style and engineering changes.

1986 Apart from the Indianapolis 500
choosing a half-ton Chevy pickup
as a commemorative vehicle for that year's race,
there was little new from Chevrolet in the truck
division in 1986. The S10 pickups saw the use of a
throttle-body fuel-injection system on the 2.8-liter
V-6 that boosted horsepower by about nine percent
to 125.

Sales continued steady at about 195,000 for the
S10, and full-size pickups rang up 438,000 in sales.

1987 This was the last year for the line
of Chevy full-size trucks that
dated back to 1973, but it also marked the first
appearance of some engineering upgrades that were
developed for the all-new 1988 pickups.

Chief among the changes was the arrival of fuel
injection on all full-size truck engines, which made
them more fuel efficient and boosted horsepower.
The system was called throttle-body fuel injection,
and it was something of a cross between a
carbureted engine and one that had true direct-to-
combustion-chamber injection. On throttle-body
injection, an electronic engine-management box dis-
penses fuel in timed bursts to injectors that are
mounted on top of the intake manifold, which mixes
the fuel and the air and sends the mixture to each

ABOVE There were two
changes that set this 1985 S10
apart from the previous year: the
hyphen was dropped from the
name and an all-new fuel
injected 92-horsepower four-
cylinder engine was made
standard. A five-speed manual
gearbox was also standard, with
a four-speed automatic optional.

RIGHT *This was the snazzy ride for a pickup cowboy in 1986: A Silverado Fleetside in red and black with the optional chrome wheel and raised white letter tires. A 5.7-liter V-8 was the popular engine choice as well.*

ABOVE *This S10 Sport model was the top Chevy compact pickup offering in 1986. The package came with five-spoke chrome wheels, chrome side rails along the cargo box and distinctive 4X4 decals on the rear fender. Although a very capable hauler, most S10s ordered this way were for commuting and weekend recreation.*

cylinder. The Chevy system used two throttle bodies to accomplish the fuel delivery, and also used an electric fuel pump mounted in the gas tank, along with a special fuel regulator.

The system allowed engine compression to be raised without causing any increase in exhaust emissions. In fact, these truck engines burned noticeably more cleanly than previous carbureted engines. Horsepower on the standard 5-liter V-8 was up to 170, and the 5.7-liter V-8 jumped to 190 hp from the 160 of the previous year. Aside from more power, these engines were smoother and had better driving characteristics than the carbureted engines, which were never particularly suited to meeting low emission regulations.

With the revised engines, Chevrolet dropped the 4.8-liter inline six and made the Vortec 4.3-liter V-6 the standard full-size truck engine. It too received throttle-body fuel injection and horsepower was rated at 160.

Other changes to the full-size line included upgrades to the electrical system, as well as minor alterations to the Silverado trim package, including a cluding a sport steering wheel and color-coordinated headliner in the cab.

The S10 continued unchanged on the outside, but received various changes in the engine compartment. The base 2.5-liter four-cylinder engine was re-designed with a new intake manifold and a cylinder head with reconfigured combustion chambers for more power and efficiency. Now called the Tech IV, its horsepower was up to 92. The optional S10 engine, a 2.8-liter V-6, was rated at 125 hp. Both engines had throttle-body fuel injection and a new single, serpentine accessory belt that replaced the multiple belts that had driven the alternator, water pump and power steering. The new belt was designed to go 100,000 miles before replacement.

In both the S10 and the full-size trucks, two-tone paint schemes remained popular options and Chevrolet offered several different ways in which the trucks could be done up.

One historical note for 1987: the El Camino model, which had seen dwindling sales for nearly a decade, quietly slipped from production after a run of more than 23 years.

1988

After nearly 70 years of building full-size pickups, Chevy's models that debuted in 1988 were as radically different as any the company had produced. Taking note of the trends over the years toward more and more women buyers, as well as the shifting of the truck market toward leisure use, Chevrolet rethought the whole pickup concept.

Although to the casual observer the 1988 trucks appeared to be just that – pickup trucks – they were actually quite different in almost all regards, and borrowed a lot of technology that had previously and successfully been introduced in the Chevy passenger car line. Even the way the trucks were built had changed. By this time new assembly lines using robotic controls assured more precise welds and greatly enhanced the fit-and-finish of the pickups – a concern that had been quite unheard of just a few years earlier in the truck-making industry.

New glass techniques allowed the use of a more sharply raked front windshield, which helped the truck's overall rounded appearance. The door glass was flush mounted, as was the rear window. Overall,

BELOW This 1987 Tahoe Sport 4X4 has a blacked out front grille and a lower front spoiler with integrated fog lamps.

there was a 33 percent increase in total window area in the cab. The doors swung open wider, the tops of the doors were cut into the roofline to create more entry headroom, and the height of the step into the cabin was lower than on previous models. This allowed much easier access than any previous model.

The chassis had new bracing that improved structural rigidity along the entire length of the vehicle; and a new coil-spring front suspension, combined with the stiffer chassis, gave the new trucks a softer ride and more precise handling.

Attention to detail was everywhere. As a way of further reducing corrosion, the truck bed was a one-piece welded unit that eliminated bolt holes that could become rust points in later years. The grille was a one-piece plastic unit that fit more tightly and put an end to lining-up problems in assembly. The front bumper also was a one-piece affair that eliminated through-the-bumper bolt holes that could be prone to rust.

The rear-mounted spare tire carrier was re-designed after years of complaints by owners. On previous models the tire was mounted under the cargo bed, and to get to it in the event of a flat it was necessary to crawl under the back end, unbolt the bar holding the tire in place, balance the tire as you lowered it down – and then repeat the dirty process when you put the tire back. On the new truck, however, Chevy took a cue from the old LUV mini truck and installed a rear tire carrier that could be lowered by a crank inserted through the rear bumper. The driver could now simply crank the carrier down and slide out the tire.

The new full-size pickups rode on the same wheelbases as the old models: 117.5 in for the base two-door pickup with the 78 in cargo box; 131.5 in with the 96 in bed; and 164.5 in for the Bonus Cab and Crew Cab trucks. Although the new models were 3.5 in narrower, the smart design of the cab resulted in more hip room, leg room and more available fore-and-after seat adjustment. The narrower design marginally reduced the cargo box width, but Chevrolet designed indentations into the box so that slats could be mounted allowing over/under stacking of such things as plywood sheets, effectively doubling the carrying capacity of the previous model.

When the new trucks debuted, the flush-fender Fleetside model was the only body style available at first. At mid-year, Chevy brought back a new version of the Step-Side body, now called the Sportside. Like the Step-Side, the Sportside retained the bulging rear fenders, but had a further addition of a rubber-clad step strip in front of and behind the fenders to help make loading easier.

A new body variation, called the Extended Cab, was offered on Fleetside models only. This version had a small storage area behind the seats and rode on

LEFT AND ABOVE The interior of the full-size Chevrolet was redesigned for the 1988 model year and the emphasis continued to be on more comfort and convenience features. On the extended cab model (left), the rear bench seat could be locked in the up position to allow for more storage space. The redesigned truck also had more glass area for better visibility. The dashboard (above) featured a full set of gauges, including a tachometer, and all radio and air-conditioning controls were within easy reach of the driver. The four-spoke steering wheel added a sporty touch.

RIGHT AND BELOW

Standard on the 1988 Fleetside was a cloth-covered bench seat that could be had in two grades of covering. The red velour-like fabric (right) was an upgrade, while the standard seat (below) had a more corduroy feel to it. A split bench seat was optional, as were bucket seats on some sport models. Power adjusters were an option as well.

a 155.5 in wheelbase. There was a fold-down, full-width bench seat at the back of the extended cab, but most users left the seat up and took advantage of the 40 cu. ft. of storage space.

Inside, the new trucks had an instrument cluster that used graphic displays for some functions, and overall trim levels were upgraded. The top-of-the-line Silverado was as luxurious as any Chevy Caprice, including such goodies as illuminated visor vanity mirrors. Just down from the Silverado was the Scottsdale package, and the Cheyenne name was resurrected for the base truck, replacing the designation Custom Deluxe. All amenities, from cruise control to power windows to power door locks to AM-FM stereo-cassette sound systems were available.

Engines in 1988 differed little from those of the previous year, but there was a significant powertrain change on four-wheel-drive models. Starting in 1988, Chevrolet began using its Insta-Trac shift-on-the-fly system on full-size pickups. This floor-mounted shifter allowed a driver to go from two-wheel-drive operation to the high-range four-wheel-drive setup at any speed. To engage the low-range four-wheel-drive – used primarily in heavy mud or very steep terrain – it was still necessary to do so from a standstill. In four-wheel-drive mode, the transfer case split the power equally between the front pair of wheels and the rear.

The S10 pickup enjoyed a new infusion of engine power with the availability of the 2.8-liter, 160 hp Vortec V-6. The three trim levels remained – Durango, Tahoe and Sport, with some upgrades to the seats, dashboard and air-conditioning controls. A special-edition model called the Back Country came with a black metal brush guard on the front grille, a bed-mounted bridge that positioned two off-road driving lamps above the cab, and other special off-road driving enhancements.

Sales of the new full-size pickups were robust — though still not enough to catch Ford. Production for 1988 was more than 514,000 for the full-size models, and the added attraction of a V-6 in the S10 helped push its sales to more than 248,000, an all-time high.

1989 So popular was the new line of Chevy trucks introduced in 1988 that by 1989 it had become (counting the clone vehicles produced under the GMC nameplate) the single biggest-selling vehicles at General Motors.

Perhaps more importantly, by 1989 the trucks were receiving glowing ratings from buyers who responded to the J.D. Power Customer Satisfaction Index survey. Buyers liked the new, smoother ride and the more rounded body styles, as well as the long list of options. A further sign of the times was that only about 20 percent of all Chevrolet trucks were being registered to companies. The rest were being bought by individuals who rarely, if ever, used them for work purposes.

Not content to rest on its laurels — and still running behind Ford in overall sales — Chevrolet made several changes to the trucks for 1989. And they included anything from adding sporty graphics to engineering improvements. Pickups that were ordered with four-wheel drive were decked out in a "4 x 4" decal scheme that helped enhance the vehicles' sporty appeal, and a Fleetside Sport model was also added. Improvements were made to the brakes to reduce squeal from the pads on the front discs, and a new shielded emergency-brake cable was fitted that was less prone to damage from stones and other road debris.

Interior upgrades included additional sound-deadening material and improved fabric and vinyl materials used throughout the three interior-trim packages — Cheyenne, Scottsdale and Silverado.

Engines and transmission remained the same on the full-sized pickups, ranging from the 4.3-liter, 160 hp V-6 to the 7.4-liter, 230 hp V-8. Most pickups were ordered with the 190 hp 5.7-liter V-8.

BELOW A special edition S10 pickup, called the Back Country, was available in 1988. The most visible addition to this truck was the aerodynamically designed light bar that was mounted in the pickup bed.

On the S10 pickup a new rear-wheel-only anti-lock brake setup was offered, and a limited-edition model that used the 1950s Cameo name appeared. The Cameo had a pseudo ground-effect lower-body skirt and other appearance add-ons. The optional V-6 was available only with the four-speed automatic transmission.

More than 521,000 full-sized pickups were sold, with S10 sales topping 228,000.

1990 Two new models of the full-size pickup appeared in 1990, and exemplified the dual nature of the U.S. pickup market.

One was called the Work Truck, and received a WT insignia on the exterior body panels. The other was called the 454SS and was aimed squarely at the buyer who wanted a truck that was just a plaything. The WT started out as a base Cheyenne model to which Chevrolet added a limited number of options they believed were popular with buyers who just wanted a pickup they could use as a heavy-duty work tool. It was available in either four-wheel-drive or two-wheel-drive configurations and in a Fleetside body style. The interior remained spartan by 1990 truck standards, and chief among the options were air-conditioning and an AM-FM radio.

BELOW *This Fleetside four-wheel-drive pickup is typical of 4x4s that were popular with a lot of recreational buyers. The gaudy logo on the side let passers-by know this was an offf-road vehicle.*

At the other end of the spectrum, the 454SS was a regular-cab, two-wheel-drive Fleetside pickup with the 230 hp, 7.4-liter V-8. The suspension was modified to improve cornering by the addition of Bilstein shocks, a heavy-duty front anti-roll bar, and a fast-ratio steering box. An oil cooler and a cooler for the four-speed automatic transmission – the only gearbox available – were included, as were 60-series tires and 15 x 7 in chrome wheels.

Inside the cab the 454SS came with high-backed bucket seats, a center console, air-conditioning, power windows and locks, a sliding rear window, and a long list of other standard features.

Interestingly, the 454SS was not a big seller, mainly because of buyer resistance to its $25,000 sticker price. Today it has become a highly collectible pickup.

Other pickups of note that year were the Z71 off-road 4 x 4 models, which were sportier-looking versions of the standard four-wheel-drive pickup.

ABOVE *A special Baja off road edition of the S10 was available in 1989. The truck came in four-wheel-drive trim with oversize knobby tires, alloy wheels, a bed-mounted light bar and a front push bar with two driving lights attached.*

BELOW *Harkening back to the famed Cameo Carrier of the late 1950s, Chevrolet resurrected the Cameo name in 1989 for this special edition sport S10, which featured a lowered suspension and a front spoiler, as well as monochromatic paint scheme.*

As an historical note, Chevrolet took a two-wheel-drive Fleetside pickup to the Indianapolis Motor Speedway and broke a record for continuous 24-hour running of a production vehicle. The pickup, equipped with a fuel-injected 5.7-liter engine, completed 993 laps at an average of 103.463 mph.

The S10 pickup started the new decade with greater availability of the optional 4.3-liter V-6 engine and the addition of Chevrolet's Insta-Trac shift-on-the-fly transfer case for four-wheel-drive models. A five-speed manual transmission was mated to the 2.8-liter V-6 only on two-wheel-drive models. S10 pickups that were 4 x 4's could be ordered with the 4.3-liter V-6 and a new Getrag-designed five-speed manual. Four-speed automatics could be ordered on both two- and four-wheel-drive S10 trucks. Inside, the instrument panel was redesigned and a line of new colors, including Garnet Red, were added.

1991 The S10 pickup received a significant facelift, with an all-new grille, emblems, body side molding and other revised trim pieces. The 4.3-liter V-6 was revised to provide smoother operation and improve reliability. Among the engine changes were tweaks to the throttle-body fuel-injection system, air cleaner and distributor. The suspension was also retuned with new front and rear shock absorbers and rear leaf springs.

A new Baja edition of the truck was offered. This was a Tahoe-trim-level S10 with high-backed bucket seats and numerous decals and insignias to gain identification with the race-prepared S10 pickups that were competing in the Baja 1000 off-road race.

The full-size pickups were basically unchanged from 1990–1 except for a few technical enhance-

OPPOSITE Fans of sheer straight-line performance found a truck that they could love in Chevrolet's 1990 lineup. Called the SS454, the Fleetside pickup came with the 7.4-liter (454-cubic-inch) V-8 in two-wheel-drive configuration. A four-speed automatic was the only available transmission. Tires were 60-series low-profile rubber mounted on alloy rims.

BELOW For 1990, the S10 pickup received Chevrolet's new shift-on-the-fly Insta-Trac system for four-wheel-drive models. The electronic system allowed the driver to select all-wheel-drive at the push of a button at any speed.

ments. The big 7.4-liter V-8 was improved using a new one-piece intake manifold and other internal changes to increase its fuel economy and reliability. For trucks that had a gross vehicle weight rating of more than 8,600 lb, Chevrolet offered the first in its series of electronically controlled automatic transmissions. Called the 4L80-E, the four-speed automatic had electronic controls that monitored both engine and transmission functions and closely matched gear and throttle demands. Other changes involved the valve train on the 5.7-liter engines, improvement to the air-conditioning controls and modification of the exterior side view mirrors.

A very weak U.S. economy, which had started to falter just after the end of the 1989 model year, had been steadily eroding all new vehicle sales. By the 1991 model year, Chevy full-size pickup sales had fallen to a little more than 404,000, with S10 sales just topping 200,000.

1992 As a way to deal with the effects of the weaker U.S. economy, Chevrolet in 1992 offered a base version of the four-wheel-drive S10 called the EL. Like the WT – or Work Truck – model offered in the full-size pickups, the EL was a base-model truck to which Chevrolet had added several popular options, such as the 4.3-liter V-6, five-speed manual transmission and power steering, and then discounted them to appeal to the

BELOW Although it sold in relatively small numbers (fewer than several thousand a year), the 454SS returned to the pickup line in 1991. It gave the entire pickup line a high-performance halo effect.

ABOVE *The Baja edition returns on a revamped S10 pickup in 1991. The S10 received a new grille and emblems, as well as revised body side moldings. The Baja edition came with the top-of-the-line Tahoe interior trim and the addition of high-back bucket seats.*

ABOVE (TOP) *Sales of the 1992 full-size Chevrolet pickup were robust, topping 450,000 units sold that year, even though there were very few changes to the truck from the previous year.*

ABOVE (BOTTOM) *The biggest interior available on a full-size Chevrolet pickup in 1993 was on the K3500 Crew Cab, a huge four-door pickup that was the most work-oriented offering in the lineup.*

Nonetheless, the interior of the K3500 was as user friendly as the smaller trucks, even down to the compact disc player mounted in the center of the dashboard.

cost-conscious buyer. Overall, there was very little that was new on the S10 for '92. Chief among the new options were high-backed bucket seats, a leather trim package and a compact disc player.

On the full-size pickups the major changes were to the heavy-duty 3500 Crew Cab model, which received many of the exterior trim changes that were first offered on all other pickups in 1988. The cab was extended for better leg room front and rear, and the wheelbase was extended by 4 in. On the Crew Cab, a new 6.4-liter turbo diesel engine was introduced with a five-year, 100,000-mile warranty.

A recovering economy helped push full-size pickup sales back above 450,000 for 1992; but S10 sales slipped to 191,000, due in large part to increased competition from the Ford Ranger and other compact pickups with new designs.

BELOW *Exterior styling changes made to the lighter-duty full-size pickups were added to the big Crew Cab Dooley in 1993. This is a two-wheel drive C3500, the largest pickup made by Chevrolet.*

ABOVE *The standard engine on the C1500 full-size truck in 1993 was this 4.3-liter V-6 that produced 160 horsepower. Next on the option list was the five-liter V-8, followed by the 5.7-liter V-8.*

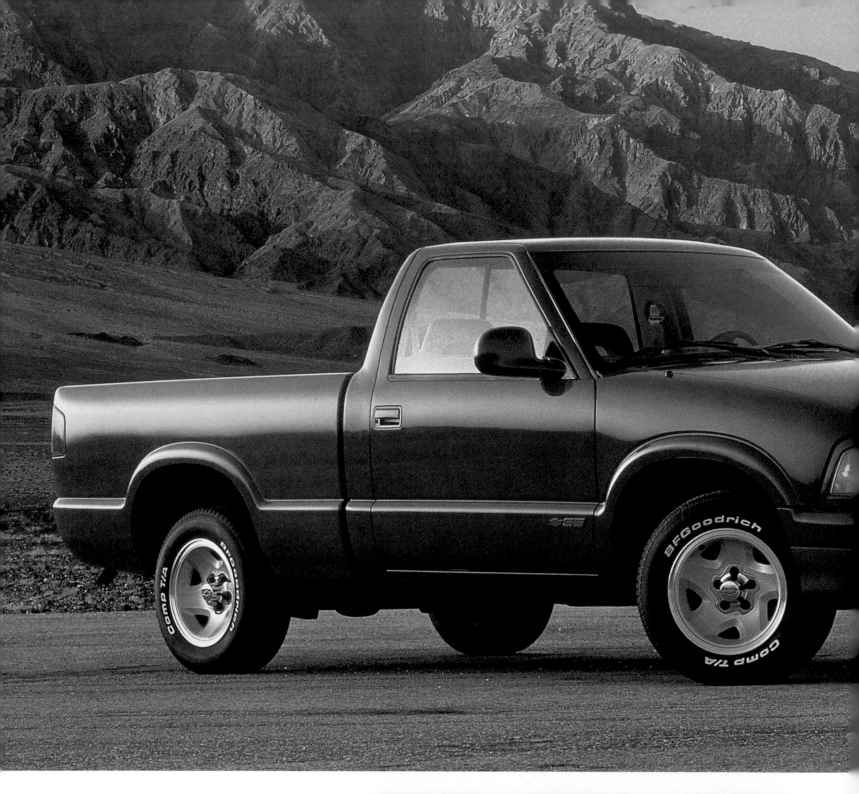

ABOVE *After seeing sales slip in the previous two years, Chevrolet unveiled an all-new S10 pickup in 1994 that was a stunningly good-looking pickup. The rounded front end and flush-mounted headlamps made the S10 very sleek. The windshield was more steeply raked for better aerodynamics and provided better cockpit visibility.*

RIGHT *Cloth and vinyl bucket seats were optional with the LS trim package. This 4X4 LS S10 is an extended cab model and has a center console.*

1993

Chevrolet continued its program of upgrades to its truck engine lineup, and for 1993 the full-size pickups benefited in a number ofl ways.

The base 4.3-liter Vortec V-6 received a new balance shaft, and all Chevy engines of 5.7-liter displacement or less were fitted with new cylinder heads, giving improved combustion. In addition there was a redesigned throttle body for the fuel-injection system. The latest in the electronic automatic transmission lineup, the 4L60-E, replaced the old four-speed automatic on all trucks with less than an 8,600 lb gross vehicle-weight rating. Trucks above that limit had first been offered with a beefier version of the electronic automatic two years earlier.

Other changes included chip-resistant paint on areas of the pickup where grit and stones were likely to hit, upgrades to the base Cheyenne interior, as well as the appearance of dual front cup holders – a first in the Chevy truck line.

1994

The big news this year was the long-overdue introduction of an all-new S10 pickup. For 1994, the S10 became larger, more aerodynamic, more powerful and more comfortable than its predecessor.

The front end was given much more rounded corners, along with a new headlamp and sidelamp treatment. The windshield was extended forward and raked for vastly increased glass area, and the side panels on the body had more flowing lines.

BELOW Improvements were more than skin deep for the 1994 S10. The optional V-6 was boosted to 195 horsepower, a new five-speed manual transmission was offered and power brakes were standard. A full anti-lock braking system was optional.

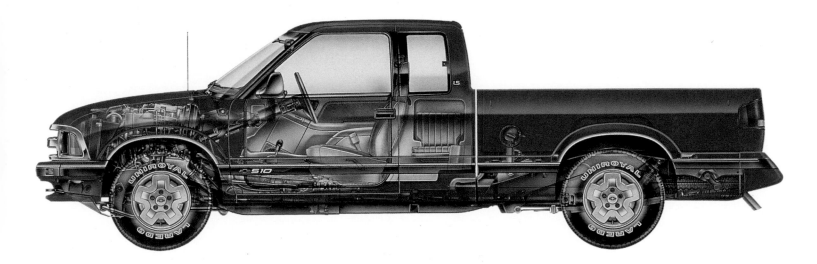

Standard Cab
vs. Crew

Since the 1970s, full-sized Chevrolet trucks have been available in several special cabin styles. By far the most common is the standard cab, which features two doors and, routinely, a bench seat that can carry three adults. A few of the sport or personal-use standard cab models will have bucket seats. No matter what the seat style, in the standard cab the seats butt up against the rear wall of the cab.

Starting in 1975, on the larger three-quarter and one-ton pickups, Chevrolet began offering what it called a Bonus Cab. This cockpit had a small area behind the regular bench or bucket seats that could be used for storage or, in some applications, was fitted with two very small jump seats for short-distance trips with four people.

In 1973, Chevrolet introduced its Crew-Cab, which had a four-door cockpit and could comfortably seat six adults. Available at first only on the one-ton chassis, it later became available also on the three-quarter-ton model.

The largest of the Crew-Cab pickups was known as the Dooley — fancifully named for the heavy-duty rear axle that carries four tires (two to a side) for better distribution of weight, particularly in towing applications. Available in the one-ton model with a 96 in. bed, a Crew-Cab Dooley rode on a massive 164 in. wheelbase and at its widest point — the rear wheel wells — was 76.8 in. across.

vs. Bonus Cab Cab Cab

CHEVROLET

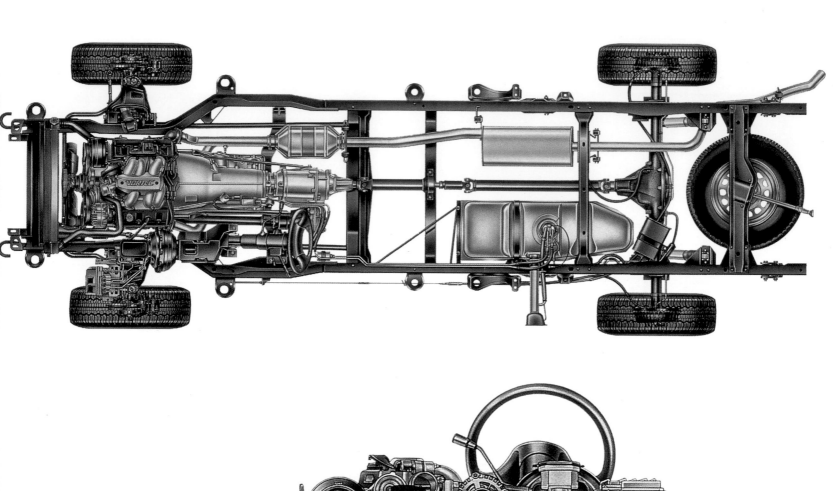

The all-new S-10 pickup was introduced in 1994, and was better than its predecessor in every way. These diagrams show the workings of the Vortec V-6 engine that was a feature of the 4.3 liter fuel-injection system.

BELOW *A new model S10 aimed at the off-road segment of the market was introduced in 1994. Called the ZR2 – the model's factory order code – it came with the Vortec V-6, four-wheel-drive, knobby tires, alloy wheels, and exterior chassis tow hooks. Either a five-speed manual or a four-speed automatic was available.*

The base engine was a 2.2-liter four that had multi-point fuel injection and produced 118 hp. The 4.3-liter Vortec V-6 discarded the throttle-body fuel injection in favor of a true port fuel-injection system that boosted output to 195 hp.

Standard equipment included a five-speed manual transmission, power brakes, power windows, and a rear-wheel anti-lock braking system. A full anti-lock system was available with the V-6 engine. A re-designed interior used a combination of vinyl and cloth coverings to give the S10 a more expensive feel.

A front bench seat was standard, with bucket seats optional. Available body styles included regular and extended cabs, with short and long cargo boxes. Cargo capacity was from 4,200 to 5,150 lb.

Two special-edition models, the Super Sport and the ZR2, were offered. The SS package included fog lamps, body-colored bumpers and grille, aluminum wheels, the 4.3-liter Vortec V-6, and a sport-tuned suspension. The SR2 was a four-wheel-drive S10 with special knobby tires, aluminum wheels, a front air dam and built-in tow hooks.

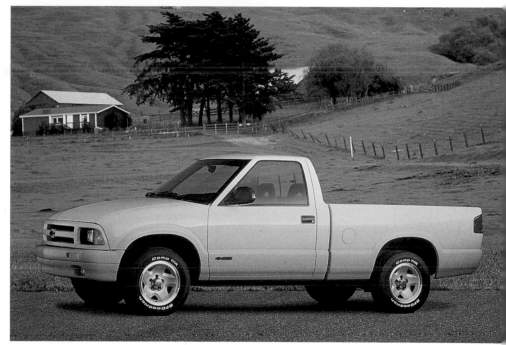

With all the emphasis (and money) put into developing the new S10, the full-size lineup continued largely unchanged for 1994.

1995

New, more comfortable interior trim packages were the big news in 1995 for Chevrolet's full-size pickups. Changes to the instrument panel offered improved air-conditioning airflow, and the texture of the carpets, headliners and seat coverings was improved. A driver's side airbag was made standard, and the center console was redesigned to incorporate a variety of surfaces that made it easier to take notes on the road.

The Z71 off-road package continued to be popular, as was a new Sportside Sport model, which had bucket seats, Bilstein shock absorbers, chrome wheels and other sportier trim options. Engines and body styles continued unchanged, although the

ABOVE *The S10 SS model attempted to capture some of the performance glamor associated with the old Super Sport models from the 1960s. It came with the 195-horsepower V-6, a sport-tuned suspension and body-colored bumpers and grille.*

exterior color lineup was expanded to include Teal Green Metallic, Autumnwood Metallic and Quicksilver metallic.

The S10, which was completely redesigned in 1994, continued largely unchanged for 1995.

1996

More power was the theme for 1996 as Chevrolet extended its Vortec name to the V-8s in the truck lineup. And it's not just a case of the same old engines with new names. In an effort to outdistance the competition, Chevrolet significantly changed the fuel-delivery systems on its three gasoline truck V-8s and brought about dramatic changes in power.

The 5-liter V-8, always a bit puny with only 175 hp, was renamed the 5000, and was uprated to 220 hp. The familiar 5.7-liter V-8 was renamed the 5700, and Vortec technology boosted power from 200 to 250. The top-gun 7.4-liter V-8 was renamed the 7400 and saw its power jump from 230 horses to 290. The new names referred to the engines' displacements in cubic centimeters.

Chevy achieved the boost in power by dumping the longstanding throttle-body fuel injection in favor of true sequential port fuel injection. Instead of having a separate injection control at each cylinder – as on the Corvette and other Chevy passenger cars – the truck engines used a new center-point injection system. The electronic control box that meters the fuel is enclosed in a two-piece inlet manifold that is part composite materials and part aluminum. Other factors that get credit for the increased power are reconfigured cylinder heads that create better fuel and air flow, and increased compression ratios, rollerized valve lifters and steel camshafts.

Thanks to sophisticated on-board electronic diagnostics, a single V-belt accessory-drive setup and other internal improvements, Chevrolet advertised that these new engines could go 100,000 miles without a major tuneup or significant service. Overall, the new engines made the 1996 Chevy pickups the most powerful and most efficient trucks it has ever built.

OPPOSITE (TOP) The S10 continued to be a hot seller for Chevrolet in 1996. This four-wheel-drive version has the short cargo bed and the regular cab. Most buyers opted for the two-wheel-drive extended cab.

OPPOSITE (BOTTOM) The biggest engine in the Chevrolet pickup truck line is the 7.5-liter V-8, which in 1996 was redesigned to boost horsepower from 230 to 290.

ABOVE Available in either the full-size pickup or the S10 in 1996, this third door on the passenger side of the extended cab made getting in and out of the rear seat much easier. There was no outside latch to the door. When the passenger door was opened, a latch on the inner door jamb would open the third door.

LEFT This 1996 extended cab S10 has the LS trim package, which included power windows, door locks, upgraded carpet and door panels, as well as other comfort items.

Driving the

Over the nine decades that Chevrolet has been building pickups, the trend toward trucks that performed in a more civilized manner – drove more easily, rode more comfortably, and offered amenities more usually found in a car – has been continuous, especially in the last 20 years.

Pickups are used more and more as substitutes for cars, rather than as brawny, no-nonsense workhorses.

But is there a pickup in the Chevrolet lineup that makes no bones about being a truck?

The answer is the Model 3500 Crew Cab Dooley. If you want a truck that can tackle just about any job without a whimper, this is your baby.

The 3500 Dooley is a two-wheel-drive one-ton pickup that has four doors, room for six adults and a 90 in-long cargo box. At the back is a rear axle with two wheels on each side, which helps to distribute the weight better when the bed is full and something is being towed at the rear.

There is no getting around it: this is one huge pickup. The overall length in 1995 trim was 249 in, overall height was more than 70 in, and the width at the truck's widest point – the bulging fenders that covered those four rear tires – was 76.8 in.

Under the hood of most Dooleys was the 7.4-liter V-8, the largest production engine in GM's light truck inventory. It was mated to an electronically controlled 4L80-E Hydramatic four-speed automatic transmission. All those cubic inches were needed because this truck was designed to carry some heavy loads. The bed was rated at a maximum of 3,900 lb, and the towing capacity was 10,000 lb – about double what the typical pickup can handle.

So how does one drive such a beast?

Carefully at first. Climbing up in the cab and settling in behind the wheel, it's easy to forget that this truck is more than 20 feet long and more than 6 feet wide. The cockpit feels much like a Chevy sedan and is every bit as comfortable for six adults. The split front bench seat is very supportive and comfortable. Controls are positioned well, and there are amenities such as cupholders and a compact disc player connected to the stereo radio.

The massive engine starts with a low, steady growl and idles smoothly. Slip the automatic in gear and you're off, thinking this is a breeze. And then you look in the mirrors and see that huge expanse of metal that seems to stretch to the horizon. Just backing out of your driveway is a major undertaking until you get the hang of it. (In fact, this truck has trouble fitting in many driveways).

On the road the ride is bouncy if there's nothing

Dooley

The Big Dog of Pickups

in the cargo bed and nothing attached to the trailer hitch. The rear suspension is set up to handle heavy loads, and when it's not weighted down it can deliver a few jolts when the pavement gets rough. But load up the cargo bed and attach a 20-foot speedboat on a tandem axle trailer, and you begin to see the best that this truck can offer. The ride smoothes out, and the truck accelerates smartly, despite the weight it's now carrying around. With a trailer hooked up, the Dooley can cruise down the freeway at 70 mph all day without breaking a sweat. Even all that length ceases to be a problem once you get used to it.

Any drawbacks? Well, fuel economy is wretched, approaching about 10 mpg under towing conditions. But Chevrolet has thought of that: the gas tank holds 40 gallons.

When the 1980 model trucks debuted, Ford was in the driver's seat when it came to pickup sales dominance. Having wrested the lead from Chevrolet in the late 1970s, Ford would keep ahead throughout the 1980s and into the 1990s.

How did Ford accomplish that feat?

Determining exactly why buyers favor one brand over another is a dicey gamble at best. Ford trucks had developed a reputation for being rugged and economical, but it's debatable how much of that was advertising hype and how much could be supported by facts. Chevrolet, for example, offered trucks that – looked at analytically – had many of the same features as the Fords, and were similarly priced. And Chevy owners were just as fiercely loyal to their trucks as Ford buyers were to theirs.

So why, consistently, have Ford trucks outsold Chevrolets for two decades?

A large part of that may have to do with the marketing of the trucks. Chevrolet has its own in-house competitor – GMC – which sells essentially the same pickup as that offered at Chevy dealerships. So it's no great leap of logic to conclude that every sale at a GMC dealer is one less sale for Chevy. Statistics seem to back this up. In 1981, for example, the combination of Chevy and GMC pickup sales would have put them about 30,000 ahead of Ford that year. Instead, Chevy came in at No. 2, about 60,000 units behind Ford.

Another factor was that Ford spent more on advertising its trucks – though Chevy was no cheapskate in this regard. The ad themes kept hammering home one message: Ford trucks were No. 1. And that undoubtedly led many people who were on the fence about whether to go with Chevy or Ford to lean in Ford's favor. Everybody loves a winner.

None of this is to say that Ford pickups, in and of themselves, weren't excellent vehicles. Ford worked hard to keep its trucks fresh and technologically advanced to protect its sales lead. Here, year by year, is how they stacked up.

1980 Ford started the decade with a re-designed pickup that differed only slightly from the 1979 model. Rather than go off on a radical tangent, Ford designers opted to continue the upright, squarish styling that had proven so successful.

BELOW Like its rival Chevrolet, Ford offered a traditional cargo bed body style that incorporated the exposed wheel wells over the rear tires. Ford called its model the Flareside. Notice the rear cargo door and its exposed rear hinges and the rubber-covered restraints, which look like they could have come off a Model A pickup.

Changes for 1980 included a new front grille that was a crosshatch of vertical and horizontal slats, single square headlamps with similarly shaped parking lights just below them. The door windows were increased in size and dipped below the level of the dashboard, giving the driver greater visibility. The cab was slightly more aerodynamic, and Ford boasted a significant reduction in drag at highway speeds, though this claim is not firmly supported.

The interiors were redone to significantly increase legroom, and the trend to more plush interiors continued with options such as bucket seats and comfortable velour fabrics on the seat cushions. Such extras as power windows, door locks, air-conditioning and several stereo options were frequently chosen options.

Ford pickups came in four ranges, two body styles, three cargo-bed lengths and two cab designs.

The base model was the F-100 Custom, which was the standard half-ton model. Next up was the F-150 Custom, which was the same as the F-100 but with power brakes and a heavier payload capacity. Next was the F-250, a three-quarter-ton pickup, and then came the F-350, which was the heavy-duty pickup rated at one-ton capacity.

The pickups could be had in two body styles — Flareside and Styleside. The Flareside had the traditional fender bulges over the rear wheels and a built-in step just behind the cab doors. The Styleside had a wider cargo box and flush rear fenders and no step. The cargo box on the Flareside was 78 in in length, while the Styleside could be had with either an 81 in or a 96 in box. Additionally, the Styleside could be ordered with a Super Cab, which provided for a small bench seat or two facing jump seats behind the front seat.

ABOVE *Ford started the 1980 model year with the most popular pickup line in America. This F-100 Custom Styleside received a minor facelift with a new front grille.*

In 1980 Ford also offered as an option a Dooley version of the F-350, which was a heavy-duty vehicle with dual rear wheels on each side of the axle for greater cargo and towing capacity.

Several trim levels above the standard Custom package were offered. Immediately above the Custom was the Ranger package, which included special body-side moldings, fancy hubcaps and upgraded vinyl seat coverings. Next up was the Ranger XLT, which added deep-pile carpeting and the option of cloth-covered seats, special inside-door trim, a cloth headliner and additional sound-deadening insulation. At the top of the list was the Ranger Lariat, which upgraded the seat coverings even further, provided greater sound insulation, and had a host of other trim changes, including special Lariat embossing on the upholstery.

For 1980 a Free-Wheeling package was also offered to give the pickups a sporty look. The suspension was slightly retuned for better on-road handling, and pin stripping, fog lamps, aluminum wheels and full gauges were included.

All Ford pickups were available with four-wheel-drive, and with a three-speed manual transmission, a four-speed manual, a four-speed manual with overdrive and a three-speed automatic.

Available engines included a 300 cu. in, 117 hp in-line six (the base motor for the F-100), a 120 hp version of the same, a 302 cu. in. V-8 rated at 130 hp, 5.8-liter V-8 developing 156 hp, and a 6.6-liter V-8 of 158 hp. All engines were carbureted and there were no diesel engines on the Ford option list, although several aftermarket companies did offer converted F-350 pickups.

Not all the engines were available in every range of pickup; the larger V-8s were confined mainly to the F-250 and F-350 trucks.

Ford's entry into the mini-pickup was the Japan-built Courier, continued unchanged since its redesign in 1977. Ford was in the process of bringing its own small pickup, the Ranger, to market, so the Courier would remain little modified until the Ranger appeared in mid-1982 as a 1983 model. Couriers were equipped with a 2-liter inline four-cylinder engine that produced 77 hp. A three-speed automatic or a four-speed manual transmission was available.

1981 There were few changes to the F-series lineup for 1981, owing in large part to the redesign that occurred in 1980. A new engine appeared on the option list, a 4.2-liter V-8 rated at 120 hp. The engine was offered for three years only as a more economical alternative to the 4.9-liter V-8 that was the staple of the Ford car and truck lineup. Few buyers ordered the smaller V-8, and in 1982 it would be supplanted by a 3.8-liter V-6.

To improve fuel economy, the automatic transmission was changed to a four-speed unit with overdrive as the top gear. The most economical engine was the 5-liter inline six, which was rated at

LEFT *Two-tone paint schemes were very popular with buyers and most opted for the contrasting color to run the length of the pickup, as it does on this 1980 F-100 Custom.*

ABOVE *A Super Cab cockpit could be ordered on the F-150, which also featured a number of upgraded trim items over the basic F-100 pickup.*

ABOVE *Ford's entry in the mini pickup category in 1980 was the Courier, which was built for Ford in Japan by Mazda. Ford owned a 25 percent stake in Mazda at the time and had been importing Couriers for eight years.*

RIGHT *A velour bench seat was optional in 1980 on the F-Series pickups, as was full carpeting, an upholstered headliner, and other nice touches. Ford trim packages were the base Custom, the Ranger XLT, and the Ranger Lariat. This truck is the Ranger XLT.*

21 miles per gallon. California air-pollution regulations were so tight, however, that this engine could not be brought into compliance. All Ford truck buyers in that state received base model pickups with the 5-liter V-8 which, because of its greater usage throughout the Ford company's model ranges, had undergone sufficiently extensive modification to meet the California standards.

The base F-100 Custom Cab received a folding seatback that allowed access to a small storage area behind the bench. Two-tone paint schemes continued to be very popular with buyers, and Ford offered at least three schemes on its F-Series pickups, ranging from a full side panel painted a complementary color to small tape stripes to accent the main body color.

The option list continued to be voluminous, ranging from a leather-wrapped steering wheel, through an AM-FM 8-Track stereo, to captain's chairs with arm rests on the Super Cab models.

1982 The way to tell a 1982 Ford pickup from a 1981 model is to look for the letters FORD on the leading edge of the hood. The letters are no longer there on the 1982 model. Starting what would be a signature styling note for all Ford vehicles, the chrome hood letters were replaced with a blue oval that had the Ford name in script, and the oval was placed in the center of the grille of all trucks and automobiles.

The other cosmetic changes for '82 involved revised nomenclature for the trim levels so as to avoid confusion with the upcoming mini-pickup, which would inherit the Ranger name. The base pick-up was called the XL, the next step up was the XLS (formerly the Ranger), which featured aluminum alloy wheels, a special tape striping scheme and a variety of comfort amenities. Top-of-the-line remained the ever-popular XLT Lariat.

The other major new option for this year was the availability of a V-6 in the base F-100 and F-150 pickups as an alternative to the 4.9-liter inline six. The new V-6 was of 3.8-liter and developed 109 hp. Despite its availability, the inline six and the 5-liter V-8 continued to be the most popular engines. Gone from the Ford lineup was the 6.6-liter V-8, banished by increasingly tighter air-pollution standards. The 5.8-liter V-8, rated at 150 hp, was now the largest engine available.

As noted, model year 1982 was the last year of the Courier mini-pickup, which disappeared about the time that the new Ranger mini-pickup was intro-duced in April as a 1983 model.

One more interesting note: owing to the popu-larity of its S10 mini-pickup and S10 Blazer, Chevrolet claimed the overall truck production title for 1982, although the Ford F-Series was the best-selling full-size pickup. Once it had brought its Ranger on-line to compete with the S10, however, Ford resumed its position as the No. 1 truck producer in America.

1983 The big news this year was the debut of the all-new Ranger mini-

ABOVE How can you tell that this F-150 Flareside is a 1982 model? Check out the Ford blue oval emblem in the center of the grille. Before 1982, the letters F-O-R-D were mounted on the leading edge of the hood. Ford adopted the blue oval emblem for all its vehicles starting in 1982.

LEFT The Super Cab F-250 was the three-quarter-ton version of the F-series and had beefier suspension than the F-100 or F-150. It also rode slightly rougher, marking it as a truck more suited for commercial uses.

ABOVE *This 1982 F-350 Dooley was the biggest hauler in the Ford lineup. The truck gets its name for the rear axle arrangement in which two tires are mounted on either side to improve load capacity. Dooleys were rated at more than 8,600-pounds gross vehicle weight.*

pickup. Larger than the Courier it replaced, the Ranger bore a striking family resemblance to the full-size F-Series trucks. Available only in a Styleside body configuration, the Ranger had a square front grille with the trademark Ford blue oval positioned to the driver's side, near the square headlamp. The Ranger logo appeared on the front fenders.

The Ranger was more than a foot shorter than the standard F-100 pickup. The Ranger's cargo box was 85 in long and 53 in wide, and it was rated for as much as 1,500-pounds carrying capacity.

Available in both two- and four-wheel-drive versions, the base Ranger had the 2-liter inline four engine rated at 72 hp. A four-speed manual transmission was standard. Optional were a 2.3-liter inline four, which produced 83 hp, and a 2.2-liter diesel four rated at 59 hp. Five-speed manual or four-speed automatic transmissions were available.

For the full-size pickups, 1983's models looked much the same as the 1982 versions. The most notable change was that the 3.8-liter V-6 and the 4.9-liter inline six traded places: the V-6 was now standard on the F-100, while the inline six was still available as an option. Also of note, a diesel V-8 was listed as an option on the big F-350 pickup. The engine displaced 7.5 liters and produced 170 hp.

1984

The Ranger styling continued unchanged, but some marketing moves were made to broaden its appeal. In addition to the base truck and the more upscale XLS and XLT models, a Ranger S model was introduced that was a very stripped-down version.

Added to the option list was a new 2.8-liter V-6 rated at 115 hp. Five-speed manual and four-speed automatic transmissions were also options.

On the full-size F-series, the F-100 model disappeared and was replaced by the F-150. In reality, there had been few differences between the F-100 and the F-150 over the preceding five years, the main ones being variations in trim and beefier rear springs to handle the larger payload capacity of the F-150.

Available in standard and Super Cab versions, the F-150 came standard with the inline 5-liter six, with the 4.9-liter and 5.8-liter V-8s as options. Gone from the full-size lineup was the 3.8-liter V-6. For fans of big V-8s, Ford introduced a 7.8-liter gasoline V-8 that produced 214 hp; it was available only on the F-250 and F-350 models.

Also new for 1984 was a four-door Crew Cab version of the F-350 pickup to compete with the similar model that Chevrolet had been offering for nearly a decade.

1985

This marked the first year that fuel-injected gasoline V-8 engines made an appearance in Ford's pickups, a trend that would eventually displace all carbureted engines. The move to fuel injection allowed not only cleaner-burning engines – critical as air-pollution standards

ABOVE *When the compact Ranger pickup debuted in 1983, it was the long-awaited replacement for the Courier. Larger than the Courier, the Ranger could carry as much as 1,500 pounds.*

OPPOSITE *At first glance it would be easy to mistake this 1984 Ranger for the full-size F-series pickup. Styling was very similar, although the Ranger was more than a foot shorter than the F-100.*

LEFT *Recognizing that the youth market was becoming very aware of small pickups as sporty vehicles, Ford offered a package on the 1986 Super Cab Ranger that included sport wheels, driving lights, and an off road rally light bar mounted in the pickup's bed.*

were raised – but higher-compression cylinder heads and greater horsepower.

A good example is that in 1985 Ford offered its venerable 5-liter V-8 in two versions. The carbureted example had a horsepower rating of 150, while the same engine with electronic fuel injection produced a stout 190 horsepower, eclipsing even the larger carbureted 5.8-liter V-8, which developed only 150 hp, but greater torque.

For those buyers who wanted the larger-displacement V-8, but with more horsepower, Ford offered a High Output version that used a single four-barrel carburetor rather than the standard two-barrel to produce 210 hp.

The Ranger model continued largely unchanged. The five-speed manual transmission became standard, replacing the four-speed manual. Sales brochures talked about the increased use of aluminum and composite materials in the construction of the pickup bed and other areas as examples of how Ford was fighting corrosion. Ford also continued to stress that the Ranger was truly a small-scale version of its F-150, down to the same ladder-type frame construction and Twin I-Beam front suspension, a Ford trademark for more than 20 years.

Sales of Ford trucks were seven percent up on 1984, with Ranger racking up more than 232,000 in sales, and the overall F-Series line accounting for an astonishing 550,000 units sold.

1986

Ranger at last followed the body lineup available on the F-Series and offered a standard cab and a new Super Cab. The Super Cab had 17 in of storage space behind the folding front seats, and two jump seats were options that could be placed back there. The Super Cab could be distinguished by the fixed-position, rectangular glass side windows. The Super Cab could be had only with the standard 72 in cargo bed, but buyers of the regular cab Ranger had a choice of 72 or 84 in cargo beds.

Under the hood, the entire Ranger engine lineup had electronic fuel injection. Base engine was the 2-liter 73 hp inline four, while the most powerful avail-

ABOVE *The 1987 lineup of full size trucks received new front and treatments that rounded off the trademark squareish look that the F Series had had since the 1960s. The headlights, grille, and turning lamps were flush mounted for better aerodynamics.*

able was a 2.9-liter V-6 rated at 140 hp. A diesel four was still on the option list, though very few were ever ordered.

On the F-150, the High-Output 5.8-liter V-8 was offered with a four-speed manual transmission as part of a sport package. Additionally, a number of items that previously had been options or part of upgraded trim packages became standard equipment. Among these were the sound-deadening insulation material, a cigarette lighter, a locking glove box and other options that in fact were being specified on virtually all the pickups sold.

1987 Ford maintained the upright, somewhat squarish look for its full-size pickups, but gave them a softer, more aerodynamic appearance through use of flush, wraparound headlamps and parking lights and a flush grille. The hood was new, as were the fenders and the front bumper with its small integral spoiler along the lower edge. The result was a very much cleaner look, without being dramatically different from the previous year's pickup. One advantage of the flush headlamps was that, when one burnt out, it was a simple matter to replace just the halogen bulb rather than the entire headlamp assembly.

An all-new interior featured vastly improved ventilation and side-window defoggers, as well as upgrades in material for the seats, door trim and headliner. Underneath, the familiar Twin I-Beam suspension remained, but there were some significant changes. A tweak to the suspension geometry

BELOW The Super Cab with its dual pane fixed rear side glass was gaining in buyer popularity. The interiors of the 1987 F-series received some ergonomic improvements to go along with the new front-end sheetmetal.

allowed more precise setting of camber and caster, always a problem with the I-Beam setup. Also, there were new V-profile accessory drivebelts on the 4.9-liter inline six and its V-8 equivalent. The base 4.9-liter six had fuel injection, pushing output to a maximum of 150 hp. Fuel injection was also added late in the model year to the big-block 7.8-liter V-8, boosting its output to 230 hp. Now only the 5.8-liter had a carburetor.

An industry first for Ford was the introduction of rear-wheel-only anti-lock brakes, which enhanced straight-line stops regardless of what was being carried in the cargo bed. Sensors monitored the velocities of the rear wheels and adjusted the braking on each accordingly. The system worked only in two-wheel-drive mode. The Flareside and Styleside body styles remain for 1987, along with the standard cab, the Super Cab and the Crew Cab. A new 4 x 4 model

for the Ranger was introduced in 1987; called the High Rider STX, it had 1.5 in more ground clearance than the previous year's 4 x 4 model. Other changes include the dropping of the 2.3-liter engine on the Super Cab models in favor of the 2.9-liter V-6. New white-painted wheels were an option on some trucks, and all the radios fitted had an electronic display, which also included a digital clock, as standard.

ABOVE *The suspension on the 1987 full-size pickups were revised so that the front I-beam set-up could be adjusted more precisely for caster and camber. Also, the engines received a single serpentine accessory belt that had a longer life expectancy.*

1988

There was one minor addition and a major deletion to the F-150 line-up for 1988. A short-wheelbase Super Cab model with a 72 in Styleside cargo bed was added, while the long-running Flareside was dropped. Ford argued that the demand for the Flareside, with a narrower cargo box than the Styleside, was limited, and the company concentrated on building as many Stylesides as possible. The decision proved somewhat shortsighted and served only to drive a few buyers to Chevrolet,

which continued to offer its similar Stepside. Clearly, there was still a significant percentage of truck buyers who wanted the traditional pickup look of the Flareside and which could not be overlooked.

The last of the carbureted pickup engines, the 5.8-liter V-8, was converted to fuel injection, and the 6.9-liter diesel was bored out to 7.3-liters. All four-speed manual transmissions were replaced by five-speed manual overdrive gearboxes.

On the Ranger, changes were limited to trim,

with new cast aluminum wheels the most visible change. A turbocharger was added to the diesel four-cylinder engine, boosting horsepower to 86 for the 2.3-liter unit.

Ranger buyers continued to be younger than the purchaser of the full-size pickup with an average age of about 30. Most buyers passed up the standard model in favor of the XLS or Super Cab models, and fewer than 20 percent of buyers used their Ranger trucks for work.

1989

The Ford Ranger got its version of some of the styling updates that appeared two years earlier on Ford's full-size pickups, the most notable ones being the flush-mounted halogen headlamps, the wraparound parking lights and flush-mounted grille.

Under the hood, a new 2.3-liter twin-spark-plug, fuel-injected inline four replaced the old four of the same capacity. The new engine developed an even 100 hp – a gain of 14 hp over the old – and had a revised intake system and distributorless ignition.

The Ranger also got the rear-wheel anti-lock braking system found on the F-Series, as well as an all-new interior featuring improved ventilation and side-window vents to cut down fogging.

To enhance driving range, a 21-gallon fuel tank was optional on the Ford Rangers that had the extended pickup bed.

On the F-Series there were very few changes in this year. The most notable was the availability of

ABOVE *Engines available on the F-series ranged from a 150-horsepower in-line six to a 230-horsepower V-8 with fuel injection. The heavier-duty trucks, like this 1987 F-250, were mostly ordered with V-8 power.*

BELOW *The Ranger received a new front-end for the 1989 model year that mirrored the rounded look given to the F-series two years earlier. The grille, headlamps, and hood were all new. Horsepower on the base four-cylinder engine was up to 100, and rear-wheel anti-lock brakes were offered as well.*

One design feature that remained popular throughout the years of truck design was the two-tone paint scheme. Other features such as the headlights, grille, tyres, and even logo changed and developed as time went on, but not this.

1987 Ford F-150

1980 Ford F-100

This shows the dash of a 1989 Ford Ranger. Options on interior for this year included padded door trims, dash-mounted ashtray and cigarette lighter, color-keyed rubber floor mat, and electronic AM radio with digital clock.

electronically controlled four-speed automatic transmissions on the heavier-duty F-250 and F-350 trucks that had gasoline engines.

The base F-150 had seen its list of standard equipment grow steadily over the years. By the end of the 1980s even the basic truck was well equipped, as the following partial list of 1989 standard items shows: front chrome bumper, tinted glass, fully padded door-trim panels, instrument-panel-mounted lighted ash-tray with cigarette lighter, color-keyed rubber floor mat, electronic AM radio with digital clock, all-vinyl folding bench seat, 150 hp, 4.9-liter inline six-cylinder engine and five-speed manual transmission. Manufacturer's list price in 1989 was $12,399.

1990

The engine and transmission packages for the F-Series pickups were improved by the widespread availability of four-speed electronic overdrive automatic transmission, which replaced the C-6 Selectshift automatic. The new transmission improved fuel economy of the V-8s and provided much smoother shifting in traffic than the old unit.

The new transmission allowed Ford to offer an electric shift-on-the-fly transfer case on its four-wheel-drive trucks. Combined with self-locking front hubs (introduced midway through 1989), the system allowed a driver to go from two-wheel to four-wheel-drive anytime he needed to, just by touching a button on the dashboard.

Other changes included the addition of a courtesy light on the cargo box, and a new com-puterized engine-monitoring system called EEC-IV, which kept a minutely detailed log of engine performance that enabled much more accurate diagnosis of any engine problems. Interestingly, the system was originally developed as a part of Ford's long and successful Formula One engine program in Europe.

For 1990 the Ford Ranger received a larger V-6 engine as an option. The 4-liter V-6 had a cast-iron block and cylinder heads, a 9-to-1 compression ratio and produced 160 hp – 20 hp more than the optional 2.9-liter V-6. Both V-6s were available in two- and four-wheel-drive versions and with a choice of either a five-speed manual or a four-speed automatic transmission.

On a limited number of Rangers with the 72 in cargo bed, Ford offered as a no-cost option a bed made from plastic composite material as a way to fight corrosion.

1991 Little was new for 1991 in the full-size pickup, as Ford, along with all other domestic manufacturers, suffered through a major sales decline and gallons of red ink on the balance sheets. Analysts said that, were it not for the high-profitability of pickups, the economic news would have been far worse in Detroit.

Availability of the electronic four-wheel-drive shift was now more widespread. The other news Ford touted was the use of double-sided galvanized steel on the doors, fenders and cargo box of the full-size pickups as a means of reducing corrosion.

Ranger added a Sport model to the lineup, offering the special tape stripe and paint package in the standard cab model only. Special aluminum alloy wheels completed the Sport truck. Elsewhere, a 60/40 split bench seat was added to the option list.

1992 Design changes to the front end of the F-Series helped distinguish them from the previous year's trucks. The aero styling that had debuted in 1988 was accentuated even further, with more shaved off the front corners and the front lip of the hood.

The biggest news was the reappearance after four years of the Flareside model to the F-150. The Flareside was a short-wheelbase pickup with the 72 in bed. Offered in both standard cab and Super Cab models, it was designed to appeal to buyers who wanted a more sporty look to their pickup than had been available up to now. In an effort to appeal to cost-conscious buyers, Ford introduced a short

wheelbase Styleside pickup called an S model that had fewer standard features and a lower price. Factory list started at $13,471.

A bookkeeping change in the way horsepower was determined resulted in an overall downgrading of horsepower numbers in 1992. The 5-liter V-8 was now rated at 185 hp, the 5.8-liter V-8 at 200, and the 7.8-liter at 230.

More standard power was top news on the Ranger. The base engine for all four-wheel-drive versions of the pickup was upgraded to the 140 hp, 2.9-liter V-6, with the 160 hp, 4-liter V-6 optional. Dropped from the 4 x 4 lineup was the 100 hp, 2.3-liter inline four.

BELOW The Flareside body style, which was dropped in 1988 and brought back in 1992, appealed to buyers more interested in a sport truck. This 1995 Flareside has optional chrome wheels and a body-colored small running board just below the door.

Elsewhere on the Ranger, Ford used additional galvanized steel to help reduce corrosion. Trim changes were made on most of the optional packages, and among these was the addition of fog lamps to the STX sport 4 x 4 Rangers. At the other end of the scale, Ford discontinued the cloth headliner on the entry-level S model as a way of reducing the price.

1993 The Ranger continued its lockstep development with the F-150, and got a new, more aerodynamic look for 1993. New flush side glass, wider doors for easier access, slight fender flares and a rounded front end were hallmarks of the freshened Ranger. As a nod to young buyers who couldn't care less about hauling anything larger than a surfboard, Ford introduced the Ranger Splash, which was a Flareside Ranger with aluminum wheels and distinctive, colorful graphics.

The 4 x 4 models got their own distinctive grille, and changes to the dashboard, seats and headliner were made to all models. The optional 60/40 split bench seats now had a center armrest, and a new multi-function control stalk was added to the steering wheel. AM-FM stereo radios with cassette or compact-disc players were offered as options.

A new 3-liter V-6 replaced the 2.9-liter V-6 that had been standard equipment on all 4 x 4 Rangers and optional on all others. The new engine produced 145 hp. The 4-liter V-6 remained an option and developed 160 hp.

There was very little change to the F-Series trucks. Some minor improvements were made to the optional cruise control, and some trim packages were consolidated or deleted from the option list.

One hot truck in 1993 was the limited edition Lightning, which was developed by Ford's Special Vehicle Operations team. The Lightning had black monochromatic paint, special wheels, fog lamps mounted in a front spoiler and a 5.8-liter V-8 that pushed out 230 hp. It was a direct challenge to Chevy's SS454, and is now a very collectible truck.

The best-selling vehicles in America — car or truck — continued to be the F-Series pickups. Three of the top 10 best-selling vehicles in 1993 were Ford trucks — the F-Series, the Ranger and the Explorer sport-utility vehicle.

1994 Safety measures that had been on passenger cars for several years began to appear on Ford trucks in 1994. On the F-Series, a driver's-side airbag was added to the steering wheel on all trucks except those with gross vehicle weight ratings of more than 8,500 pounds. Also, side-door impact beams were installed for added security in collisions, and a brake/shift interlock system was added to pickups equipped with automatic transmissions. The brake interlock prevented the driver from shifting from park into reverse or drive without having his foot on the brake pedal. Another safety feature was a center high-mounted taillight, mounted at the top rear of the cab.

For buyers who opted for a diesel engine, Ford offered a turbocharged version of its 7.3-liter V-8 that produced 190 hp. Although rated at only 5 hp more than the naturally aspirated version of the same engine, the turbo gave the diesel a wider power band for smoother operation under heavy loads. Other Ford engines received minor improvements such as changes to pistons, camshaft rollers and engine materials that resulted in minor increases in fuel mileage.

Air-conditioning units on the F-series were of a new design that used the refrigerant R134a, which was free of chlorofluorocarbons found in the old R12 refrigerant that had been the industry standard for decades. Some scientific evidence indicates that chlorofluorocarbons deplete the earth's protective ozone layer.

A comfort feature that debuted in 1994 was a "40/20/40" bench seat that gave the driver and the outboard passenger their own seats with individual recliners and power lumbar adjusters, while retaining a center area that, with the padded armrest and storage bin folded, made room for a third passenger.

Ranger added a Super Cab 4 x 4 version of its Splash pickup that proved very popular with young buyers, who saw the compact pickup as something akin to a sports car. Advertising for the Splash played up the surfboard-in-the-back theme and made no mention of the truck's hauling abilities.

1995

A new top-of-the-line trim option was added to the F-Series in the form of the Eddie Bauer Edition, named for the fashionable outdoor clothier, featuring a two-tone paint scheme, the Eddie Bauer logo on the exterior and the interior, and upgraded seat coverings.

Otherwise, the F-Series was little changed. The turbo diesel engine introduced a year earlier, called the Powerstroke, became the sole diesel offering, and was available with a choice of either automatic or manual transmission.

On the Ranger, a driver's-side airbag was added, as was a brake/shift interlock on automatic transmission models. A four-wheel antilock brake system was now standard on Rangers with the 4-liter V-6 and all four-wheel-drive models, and available as an option on all other Rangers.

The 2.3-liter four and the 3-liter V-6 received minor internal improvements that made them run more smoothly and boosted power by up to 10 hp. An improved electronically controlled four-speed automatic was also available.

On the outside, Rangers got a new grille, while inside there was a redesigned instrument panel. Optional on Super Cab models was a six-way power seat, and a six-disc compact disc player and remote entry/alarm setup were available on all models.

ABOVE *In 1995, Ford offered a turbocharged diesel engine called the Powerstroke in 1995 F-series pickups. The engine, which featured extraordinary low-end torque, was ordered mostly by buyers of the F-350, like this Dooley, who expected to put a lot of miles on their truck in long-haul situations.*

ABOVE *The F-series Styleside Super Cab was the most popular body style among buyers in 1996. Creature comforts that were available included power leather seats, power mirrors, power windows, power door locks, and a compact disc player.*

1996

This became the last year for the F-Series design, which debuted in 1980 and was, by all sales measures, a smashing success for Ford. With a 1977 model due out in January 1996, the 1996 pickup was a transitional vehicle. While Ford slowly changed over its production lines in the United States and Canada to the new-generation F-series, the 1996 model was to continue in production until late in the year so that buyers would have a choice of the old and new styles.

Very few changes were made to the 1996 model. Some wood trim appliqués were added to the Eddie Bauer models, integrated head restraints were added to the front bench seat, and improvements were made to the hub-locking system and transfer case on four-wheel-drive models, generally, for better reliability and durability.

Ranger got the added safety feature of an optional passenger-side airbag. As an added precaution, the passenger airbag could be deactivated by a dashboard switch if a rear-facing child safety seat was in use. Studies have shown that airbags can injure infants in such seats, and the dashboard deactivation feature is an industry first.

Other changes included a factory certification of all Ranger engines stating that they can go 100,000 miles between tuneups under normal driving conditions together with regular fluid and filter changes. The Flareside body style, previously available only with the Splash trim package, is now offered with other trim levels as well.

1997

Ford was rolling the dice in a big gamble with its next-generation F-Series pickup. The first redesign for the F-Series since 1980, the new trucks were as bold a statement as Ford had ever made. Based in part on the Triton show truck that made the rounds in 1995, the new F-150, had a rounded yet muscular look to it. The aluminum hood sloped sharply away from the cockpit, and the round mouth of the grille is a sharp departure from the 1996 truck.

The side panels on both the Styleside and the Flareside were voluptuous, especially on the Flareside, and made the truck seem smaller than the one it replaced, although in fact it is larger in almost all

OVERLEAF *The Ranger line was mostly unchanged for 1995, but it still was wildly popular with buyers. It ranked in the top five of all vehicles sold in the United States that year.*

ABOVE *After nearly 17 years without major changes, the F-series that buyers had made No. 1 in the United States was being phased out for an all-new 1997 model. The 1996 models were largely unchanged from 1995, but because of a slow changeover to the new truck they were built and sold well into the 1997 model year.*

dimensions. The wheelbase was 5.5 in longer and overall length was up to 7.5 in greater, depending on which pickup bed was used. Payload on the standard F-150 was a whopping 2,435 pounds.

Ford said it wanted the new truck to shout ruggedness, yet also to look refined. The company will try to attract more leisure buyers – the heart of the Chevy sales core – while holding on to its loyal band of commercial buyers.

Two areas where Ford made mechanical changes could have a bearing on this. One was the huge decision to discard the Twin I-Beam front suspension that Ford had been using since the 1960s. The suspension had gained a reputation for toughness, particularly in off-road use, but it didn't ride or handle as well as a more conventional coil spring arrangement. In the 1997 F-Series Ford opted to go with a more traditional Short/Long A-arm front suspension with coil springs on two-wheel-drive versions and torsion bars on 4 x 4 pickups.

The new suspension rides more smoothly and steers more easily than the old design, and, to allay fears that it might not be as durable, Ford made the upper arm control arms from forged steel and set a target of 150,000 miles or 10 years usage without major repairs.

The other area of interest was the decision to go with an overhead camshaft V-8 as the base V-8. Commercial truck buyers have long held that the more conventional pushrod V-8s were more reliable and cheaper to maintain and repair than ohc engines. The base V-8 in the 1997 F-150 was a 4.6-liter single-overhead-camshaft V-8 – one of the modular

V-8 engines that first appeared on Lincolns and Ford Crown Victorias. It was the first application of this technology on a production pickup. Ford engineers have set up the 210 hp engine so that it will go 100,000 miles before needing a tuneup, and they believe it will get better gas mileage than a comparable pushrod V-8. A 5.4-liter version of the new engine was slated to appear, and perhaps in 1998 a V-10 will be offered in the F-350.

The base engine in the '97 F-150 was also new — a 4.2-liter 205 hp V-6 developed also for the Taurus sedan; it too was rated at 100,000 miles before the first major tuneup.

Another new feature was the introduction of a third door on the Super Cab models. Located on the passenger side of the truck, the third door offered much easier access to the rear seat or storage area. (Chevrolet, in an attempt to beat Ford to market, began offering a similar door in 1996).

The new truck was at first limited to the F-150; in 1998 similar F-250 and F-350 pickups will be introduced. During the changeover period, the old F-Series design will be offered in showrooms alongside the new model, giving buyers a unique opportunity to decide for themselves whether they prefer the more staid look or the power bulge style.

BELOW Harkening back to a day when pickups more closely resembled their big-rig cousins, Ford made a bold styling statement with the all-new 1997 F-150. The front end has a very brawny look. Underneath, there is an all-new suspension that uses conventional coil springs and shocks as opposed to the twin I-beam setup that Ford used for more than three decades.

Taking A

I f there ever was a pickup that deserved to be compared to a sports car, it's the Ranger Splash. Conceived as a vehicle targeted at buyers in the 18–30 age bracket, the Splash is a saucy truck that does a variety of things well and provides a good time as well.

Equipped with the powerful 160 hp, 4-liter V-6 and four-speed automatic transmission, a two-wheel-drive Splash accelerates smartly, going from zero to 60 mph in a very respectable 8 seconds.

Equipped with the 15-in aluminum-styled wheels and the 215-75/15 all-season radial tires, the Ranger Splash does a very good job of taming most corners. The recirculating-ball-type power steering is not as precise as rack-and-pinion, but it provides honest feedback that builds driver confidence. The conventional arrangement of coil springs at the front and leaf springs at the back gives the Splash a firm but not bone-jarring ride that is not unlike some models of the Mustang. Understeer is there, but it's predictable and most driver's won't find its limits.

The two-seat cockpit on a bucket-seat equipped standard cab Splash looks for all the world like the interior of a sports car. The seating position is more upright, but there is a sporty feel to the controls and the exterior view is excellent. if there wasn't a cargo bed out back, the illusion would be complete. But of course there is a cargo bed on the Splash — and that makes it a very versatile vehicle. The bed measures 71.8 in and can carry 1,050 lb of whatever you need hauled.

But it's doubtful if many Splashes are sold with the idea they will spend much time lugging junk around. They're too much fun for that kind of drudgery.

Dip *in the Splash*

chapter 5

Dodge

The fact that there are new Dodge trucks on the road today is something of a commercial miracle. Historically the corporations of General Motors, Ford, and Chrysler (Dodge's parent company) were called The Big Three of automobile manufacturing.

However, in reality, for the last 40 years it has been The Big Two and a Half, because Chrysler has never had the product or financial base to compete with Ford or GM. Chrysler's market share in the 1960s — both cars and trucks — was never much above 10 percent, if that, and it was always struggling from one financial crisis to the next.

Then came the triple whammy of the 1970s: gasoline shortages created by the Arab oil embargo; unexpectedly strong competition from the Japanese; and demands from the federal government that all cars be fitted with expensive safety and anti-pollution equipment. The effect on Chrysler was devastating, and it seemed to be compounded by a management team that was doing an excellent imitation of an ostrich. By the late 1970s Chrysler was effectively bankrupt and most analysts expected that sometime soon it would close its doors or be bought out by Ford, General Motors or a foreign carmaker.

Then, in an amazingly astute move, the Chrysler board of directors hired Lee Iacocca to try to save the company. Iacocca had been let go as president of Ford in the late 1970s in what almost all industry observers agree was a battle of titanic egos. Iacocca had an impressive track record at Ford, and his most notable accomplishment there was the introduction of the phenomenally successful Mustang in 1964. He kept Ford profitable and competitive with the much larger General Motors, and was seen as a sure and

natural successor to Henry Ford II as chairman of the board of directors.

Iacocca's downfall at Ford seemed to stem from repeated run-ins with Henry Ford II over exactly whose company it was. Henry Ford II — grandson of the original Henry Ford — also had a huge ego, and eventually it became apparent that there wasn't room at the top for both men. And, since the company was named Ford, Iacocca was the man who left.

It may well have been the best thing to ever happen to him. He became a legend for saving Chrysler. In 1981, when Chrysler was just weeks from being forced to close down, he persuaded the federal government to stand behind $2 billion in loan guarantees he said were needed to tide the company over until he could revamp Chrysler's sorry lineup of cars and trucks. Then, Iacocca wrung from the United Auto Workers unprecedented concessions on wages, benefits, work rules and staffing by, among other things, putting the union president on the board of directors, in essence making the union a business partner. Iacocca also made huge cuts to the white-collar ranks at Chrysler, and set a standard that said you had to be productive to survive at the new Chrysler Corporation.

Then he went on television and to act as personal pitchman for Chrysler, becoming a national celebrity whose name and face were more familiar than those of many government leaders.

Adventurer SE

Adventurer SE

Adventurer Sport

Custom Sweptline Pickup

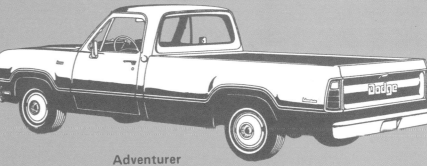

Adventurer Sport

Custom Sweptline Pickup

Adventurer

Adventurer

Utiline Pickup

Utiline Pickup

IMPORTANT: USE TRUCK ORDER
FORM IN THIS BOOK TO SECURE
TRUCK MATS OR SLICK PROOFS.

D200 Sweptline Crew Cab

D200 Sweptline Crew Cab

ABOVE AND OPPOSITE *Dodge pickups in 1980 came in two models. One was the Utiline, with its exposed rear wheel wells, and the other was this Sweptline Custom, with its smooth-sided cargo box.*

The combination of all these elements — combined with an upswing in the national economy that began in 1983 — worked to revive Chrysler to the point where, in terms of efficiency of operation, the company was a model for a while in the industry. And the $2 billion loans were paid in two years.

What did all this mean for the Dodge truck lineup?

In the beginning, and for too many years afterward, it didn't mean much. Chrysler (Iacocca, really) knew that to get the company on an even keel it had to build vehicles for the masses, and trucks — although getting more popular — wouldn't fit the bill. Also, the stranglehold that Ford and Chevrolet had on the full-sized pickup market looked too strong to put a dent in.

So for much of the 1980s Chrysler concentrated first on its passenger sedans, introducing the K-car platform in 1982, an economical setup that was very versatile. Then, in 1984, came the trump card in Chrysler's comeback poker game: the minivan. Although the minivan genre is classified as a truck, in fact the original minivan was based on the K-car platform and contained no parts from the Dodge truck lineup. This was probably a good thing, because Chrysler had last made serious, significant changes to its truck lineup way back in 1972, and the next complete redesign and re-engineering effort wouldn't come until an all-new truck was introduced in 1994. So overdue was the new truck that the old model was jokingly called "Grandpa" by Chrysler designers and engineers because of its longevity.

That doesn't mean there weren't good Dodge trucks built between 1980 and 1994. Although not leaders in style or innovation, Dodge trucks had a solid reputation for reliability and toughness that dated back to World War II. And some of the mini pickups that Dodge introduced in the 1980s — the D50, the sporty Rampage and the Dakota — were very popular with buyers who were willing to pass up Ford and Chevy and take a look at Dodge.

1980 Dodge began the 1980s with two body styles and three payload levels on its full-size pickups. The pickups were designated the D150 (half-ton), D200 (three-quarter ton) and D300 (one ton), with four-wheel-drive available in all three capacities.

When the four-wheel-drive system was specified, the designations were W150, W200 and W300. The Power Wagons, as the four-wheel-drive pickups were known, were significantly changed in 1980. Until that year, the Power Wagons had used full-time four-wheel-drive setups, which tended to be noisier and used more fuel than equivalent two-wheel-drive models. The new system followed the lead of Ford and Chevrolet and was an on-demand drivetrain that allowed the driver to shift from two-wheel-drive operation to four-wheel-drive at rest or in motion. The result was a much more versatile system that was also less costly to service than the old setup.

Full-size pickups were offered in Utiline and Sweptline styles. The Utiline was Dodge's version of the Stepside and Flareside pickups from Chevrolet and Ford. It had the more traditional rear cargo box with flares over the rear wheels and a built-in step just behind the passenger cab. The Sweptline had smooth fenders on the cargo bed, and also was offered in Club Cab versions that had a small storage or short-haul passenger compartment behind the front seat. A four-door Crew Cab model was offered on the D300.

The standard pickup bed was 78 in long, with a 96 in bed optional on Sweptline models only.

The engine lineup began with the venerable 225 cu. in. Slant Six, which was a Chrysler exclusive design. It was a carbureted inline six with the bank of cylinders canted slightly to the right, and for the pickups it received solid valve lifters, four main bearings and shot-peened rods. Horsepower in 1981 was rated at 110.

The base V-8 was a 318 cu. in. version with five main bearings, hydraulic valve lifters and a two barrel carburetor. It was rated at 145 hp. The other engine available was a 360 cu. in. V-8 that also had five main bearings and hydraulic lifters. The larger V-8 produced 160 hp and used a four-barrel carburetor.

Transmission choices were a four-speed overdrive manual and a three-speed automatic.

Trim levels for the full-sized pickups started with the base Custom, which was a bare-bones truck that had rubber floor mats instead of carpeting, and ran up the scale from Adventurer to Adventurer Sport to the top-of-the-line Adventurer SE.

The Adventurer series added a variety of tempting interior and exterior accouterments, from quad headlights with chrome accents, to sport wheels, carpeting, fabric headliner, upholstered door panels, several different grades of vinyl on the bench

seats, and radio options. Other extra-cost options included air-conditioning, power windows, and power steering. The other pickup in the Dodge stable in 1980 remained the D50, a mini-pickup that Dodge bought from Mitsubishi and renamed. The D50 first appeared in 1979, and for 1980 remained largely unchanged. The base model had a 2-liter inline four that produced 93 hp and was connected to a four-speed manual gearbox. It had a 78 in cargo bed, and a rated carrying capacity of 1,400 lb. The other current model was called the Sport; it had a 2.6-liter inline four rated at 105 hp and came standard with a five-speed manual transmission.

Both models could be ordered with a four-speed automatic transmission, and standard equipment included a 15.1 gal fuel tank, dual exterior rearview mirrors, a color-keyed cloth headliner, tinted glass, an AM radio and an adjustable steering column. The

D50 trucks had carlike A-arm front suspensions and leaf rear springs. The ride was quite good for a pickup, and the Sport model, which had bucket seats and was often ordered with a bed-mounted light bar and custom wheels, was popular among younger buyers. Color choices were somewhat limited. The standard D50 came in white, tan and black. Other colors available on the Sport model were orange, yellow and a bright blue.

Dodge trucks suffered mightily in the sales race. Although the overall truck industry was down significantly, Dodge was hit hardest. Production of light-duty pickups dropped by more than 60 percent, and overall Dodge sold just 119,000 trucks.

1981 The hallowed Dodge model name Ram was added to the D50 pickup, although little else changed. The base mini pickup was now called the Ram 50 Custom, and the Sport model was now called the Ram 50 Sport. A third model, the Ram 50 Royal, was created in 1981; it had a few more interior trim upgrades than the standard Ram 50 Custom, and came with the larger 2.6-liter four-cylinder engine. The Ram Sport 50 came standard with high-backed bucket seats, a center console, five-speed manual transmission and spoked road wheels. The full-size pickup was freshened slightly, with a new, more rounded front end that featured a restyled chrome grille, recessed single-lens

headlights, and changes to the side trim and marker lights. The instrument panel was redone, and the vinyl bench seat was available in four colors: blue, black, tan and red. Standard equipment included a 20 gal fuel tank, front disc brakes, color-coordinated interior door panels and arm rests, black rubber floormat with padding, dual exterior rearview mirrors, AM radio and hubcaps.

Dodge also offered its pickups with several special-duty body packages. One was called the SN-Commander, and was equipped with an angled snow-plow blade mounted to the front. The blade could be raised or lowered from the cockpit using special controls and could deal with substantial snow drifts. Also offered was the Retriever Wrecker, a factory built tow truck. A dual-rear-wheel package called Dyna-Trac was available, and boosted total gross vehicle weight capacity to 10,000 lb.

Also in 1981 Dodge decided to change the name of its pickup trim packages. The Adventurer series was replaced by the Custom SE, which featured exterior chrome trim and a side plate with the leaping Ram symbol on it; the Royal, which added interior trim upgrades such as carpeting on the lower portion of the doors; and the Royal SE, which added a chrome Ram's head hood ornament and wood door-trim appliqués.

A sport trim model, called – believe it or not – the Macho Package, added bold exterior stripes, a two-tone paint scheme, special wheels and a bed-mounted light bar.

1982 The big truck news for 1982 was the debut of the Rampage, the first front-wheel-drive pickup offered by a major American manufacturer. The Rampage was based on the Dodge Charger sport coupé, and in spirit could be said to have its roots in the marketing philosophy that created the Chevy El Camino and the Ford Ranchero of the 1950s and 1960s.

The Rampage was more car than truck, retaining virtually the same suspension and drivetrain that the Charger offered. The engine was a 2.2-liter four-cylinder that was the staple of the K-car line. It put out 84 hp and could be had with either a four-speed manual transmission or a three-speed automatic gearbox. The front suspension was a McPherson strut arrangement and the overall construction was a unibody design, unlike the traditional pickup mode of a ladder frame with a separate body.

The Rampage was offered in two trim levels, the High Line and the Sport, with the latter proving more popular with buyers. Cargo capacity was about 1,000 lb, but it's doubtful if it could comfortably carry that much in its 60 in bed.

For people who wanted a more conventional – and practical – minitruck, Dodge continued to offer the Mitsubishi-based Ram 50, the styling of which was mostly unchanged from 1981. One major new

BELOW *A short pickup bed helped give the D-150 Sweptline something of a jaunty look. Pin stripe and full wheel covers also help.*

option, however, was the addition of a four-wheel-drive model, which was available in the base Ram 50 or Ram 50 Sport. The Ram 50 trucks outsold the Rampage model by a two-to-one margin.

There were no changes to the full-size pickup except for the addition of a special stripped-down price leader model called the Miser, which carried a list price that was about $720 below that of the entry-level D150 Sweptline.

1983

Throughout the Dodge truck line-up there were virtually no changes this year, reflecting Chrysler's push to shore up its passenger-car lineup and devote its resources to the coming minivan.

The major news was that starting midway through the model year, Dodge began offering as an option a 5.9-liter inline six diesel engine built by Cummins, the internationally respected maker of

diesels for big-rig commercial trucks and off-road dumpers. The engine was turbocharged and produced 160 hp. It proved very popular with commercial pickup buyers because of its durability and the traditional longevity of diesel units.

A curious fact is that it was cheaper in 1983 to buy a full-size Dodge pickup than one of the mini pickups. Base price of a Rampage was $6,683, and $6,266 on a Ram 50, while a full-size D150 Miser pickup was $5,989. Of course, the D150 Miser lacked almost all the creature comforts, such as carpeting, padded door panels, radio and other features, that were standard on the Ram 50 and the Rampage.

Sales that year somewhat reflected the bargain nature of the base D150. More than 60,000 D150s were sold, compared to more than 29,000 Ram 50s and 8,000 Rampages. When the heavier-duty D250 and D350 trucks were included, pickup sales for 1983 were more than 112,000.

ABOVE *With its 2.2-liter four-cylinder engine and front-wheel-drive chassis, the Rampage had more in common with the company's passenger cars than with its trucks.*

ABOVE *Quad headlamps and a body-coloured grille were the first major styling changes to the Rampage.*

1984 The Rampage received a new front-end treatment that further emphasized its sporty nature. Four rectangular headlamps combined with a slotted body-color grille and a new hood to give it a more aggressive look. A five-speed manual transmission was now standard, with the three-speed TorqueFlite automatic as an extra-cost option.

Sales would hit more than 11,000 units in what would be the last year of Rampage production. Room on the assembly line and in dealer showrooms would be given over to the new Dodge minivan, which used many of the same components found under the hood of the Rampage.

The Ram 50 compact pickup continued unchanged for 1984 except for a $500 cut in the base price of the entry-level Custom model, which helped it compete better with Toyota and Nissan. On four-wheel-drive models automatically locking front hubs were added, making it possible for a driver to go from two-wheel to four-wheel-drive and back just by moving the gearshift lever. Before, a driver had to get out of the truck and manually lock the front hubs for four-wheel operation.

A new D100 model was added to the full-size pickup line, and served as the entry-level model. It was available only in the smooth-sided Sweptline style, and its cargo capacity was about 1,000 lb less than that of the D150, which remained in the lineup, along with the D250 and D350. The D100 was available in two- and four-wheel-drive versions, and was priced about $700 less than the D150.

1985 The Rampage was dropped from the pickup line for 1985, leaving the Ram 50 as Dodge's sole offering in the compact pickup market.

The Ram 50 received a new grille, which featured thin rectangular slots and a blacked-out appearance, combined with recessed quad headlamps. The base engine was a 2-liter four that produced 90 hp. A 2.6-liter four rated at 104 hp was optional. A 2.3-liter turbocharged diesel four was also listed on the option sheet, but no production figures were available at the time of writing.

On the full-size pickups, there were no significant changes, as Chrysler continued to spend its development money elsewhere. Nonetheless, a strong U.S. economy pushed Dodge pickup sales to more than 220,000, including more than 66,000 of the Mitsubishi based Ram 50.

1986 Minor grille changes were again made to the Ram 50, and the Royal trim model – which had been slotted between the base Custom and the top-of-the-line Sport – was dropped, as was the turbo diesel model that had appeared in 1985. Four-wheel-drive was available on both Custom and Sport models.

B E L O W *The Rampage had a new look for 1984, with an emphasis on its sporty appeal.*

ABOVE *The 1986 Dodge Ram 50 Sport received minor grille changes that year. The diesel engine was dropped from the lineup and four-wheel-drive was available on all models.*

The full-size pickups received new chrome grilles that featured four long rectangular slots and single round headlamps mounted in rectangular chrome slots. The available engines continued to be the 3.7-liter Slant Six, rated at 95 hp; the 5.2-liter V-8, which produced 135 hp; and the 5.9-liter V-8, which put out 185 hp. All three engines were carbureted.

1987 This was the year that Dodge introduced the all-new Dakota, which filled a niche between the full-size Ram models and the Ram 50 compact pickups that Dodge bought from Mitsubishi. The Dakota was meant to compete with the Chevrolet S10 and the Ford Ranger, but it was slightly bigger than either of those trucks and therefore occupied a market segment that it had basically all to itself.

Dodge offered the Dakota in two sizes: the first had a 111.9 in wheelbase with a 78 in pickup bed; and the second had 123.9 in wheelbase with a 96 in cargo bed. It was offered in two-wheel- and four-wheel-drive models, and the smooth-sided Sweptline cargo bed was the only style available. Overall, the Dakota looked very much like a three-quarter-size version of the D100 standard pickup, but with a slightly sportier flair.

The base engine was a 2.2-liter inline four that produced 90 hp and came standard with a five-speed manual transmission. The only optional engine was a 3.9-liter V-6 that in essence was the 5.2-liter V-8 with two cylinders removed. It was rated at 125 hp. A five-speed manual gearbox was standard, with a three-speed automatic optional.

The front suspension on the Dakota was the first fully-independent setup used on a Dodge pickup, excluding the car-based Rampage and the Mitsubishi-based Ram 50. The new suspension gave the Dakota a much softer ride, but the payload capacity was still 1,250 lb, with rear spring options that would boost that carrying capacity to 1,800 or 2,550 with the V-6. Late in the year, Dodge revised the payload capacity options and made 1,450 lb the standard V-6 rating and the optional setup was tagged at 2,000 lb.

The basic trim levels of the Dakota included tinted glass, a cloth interior headliner and sound insulation, rubber floor mat, a vinyl bench seat, and AM radio. The upgraded SE model came with carpeting, a cloth and vinyl bench seat and other comfort features. The option list on the Dakota was extensive, reflecting the marketing strategy that positioned the Dakota as a pickup that would appeal to buyers who wanted more than just a work vehicle.

On the full-size pickups there were very few changes. A new clearcoat paint process improved the finish of the trucks, and a new base coat helped the paint resist chipping. On LE models there was a new pecan-style wood appliqué on the dashboard, and a flow-through fresh-air vent system was standard.

1988

Fuel injection was added to the 5.2-liter V-8 in the full-size Ram in the form of a throttle-body system. It helped boost horsepower by 17 percent to 140 while improving driveability and reducing exhaust emissions. The base 3.7-liter Slant Six continued as a carbureted engine, as did the optional 5.9-liter V-8.

Fuel injection also was added to the 3.9-liter V-6 in the Dakota, making it a much smoother-running engine, although horsepower remained at 125. Also, the three-speed automatic transmission was replaced by a four-speed model.

A new model was added to the Dakota line, called the Sport. It was available in only three colors – red, white and black – and featured a front air dam with fog lights, a bed-mounted light bar with off-road spotlights, an AM-FM stereo radio with cassette tape player, full carpeting, a fold-down center arm rest and dual remote-control rear mirrors.

1989

A new base engine was now added to the full-size pickup, the 3.9-liter fuel-injected V-6 previously offered in the Dakota.

BELOW In its most basic form, the Ram 50 was a good, economical truck. But it soon would give way to the more advanced and larger Dakota mid-size pickup.

Dodge had come a long way by the early nineties, particularly with the arrival of the Dodge Ram, which was a mean machine compared to the more aerodynamic mid-eighties models. It was so popular that it catapulted Dodge into the front line as far as trucks were concerned. The V-10 option made it a pretty serious truck, as did the comfort of the interior, with plush seating and plenty of leg room.

1995 Dodge Ram Club Cab

1996 Dodge Ram Club Cab

1986 Dodge D150 Custom

Throttle-body fuel injection was also added to the 5.9-liter V-8, which raised output to 190 hp. The 5.2-liter V-8 model had received fuel injection the previous year.

The other major improvement for 1989 was the addition of a computer-controlled rear-wheel anti-lock braking system as standard equipment, and the availability on four-wheel-drive Ram 250 and 350 four-wheel-drive models of a 5.9-liter Cummins turbo diesel six.

There were several mechanical improvements to the Dakota in 1989, but the most exciting news was the addition of a convertible model and a special, limited edition Shelby performance model that featured a V-8 that had been modified by famed race-car builder Carroll Shelby.

The convertible was an industry first. It essentially was a Dakota Sport model with the cab roof chopped off and a folding canvas top substituted. Unlike a car, which depends on the roof for structural rigidity, a pickup uses body-on-frame construction that doesn't depend on the body shell. So making a convertible of a pickup is in fact easier to do than to make a ragtop out of a regular car. In fact, customizers in California had been making convertible conversions for small Japanese pickups for years, and that is undoubtedly where Dodge got the idea originally.

The Shelby model arose out of Carroll Shelby's longstanding relationship with Lee Iacocca. He had already done some special-edition cars for Dodge to help its performance image. The truck was the last in that lineup and featured the 5.2-liter V-8 with some special Shelby tweaks, including dual exhausts. Horsepower was rated at 210, and it was available only with an automatic transmission and in two-wheel-drive form. Both the Shelby and the convertible had limited-productioin runs and only a few thousand of each were sold.

Buyers of more mundane Dakota pickups saw improvements to the 5.9-liter V-6 in the form of better lubrication and a revised intake manifold. Horsepower remained unchanged, but throttle response was vastly improved.

LEFT *The convertible Dakota pickup was a Dodge original. It sold well in California, but had limited appeal elsewhere and disappeared from the lineup after just three seasons.*

1990
This was a very static year for Dodge trucks. Very few changes occurred in the Dakota lineup, with both the

LEFT *The last of the old pickups, this 1991 Ram was the last model to receive a cosmetic makeover before the all-new model appeared in 1994.*

BELOW *The totally redesigned 1994 Ram was the saving grace for Dodge's pickup line, as the full-size trucks had become very stale.*

convertible and Shelby models carrying over for one more year. The major novelty in 1990 was the introduction of a Club Cab model for two-wheel-drive pickups. The new body style was built on a 130.9 in wheelbase, and featured a small rear seat that had two storage areas hidden under the lower cushion. The cargo box on the Club Cab model was 78 in long.

There were no discernible changes to the full-size pickups in this year

1991

A minor facelift was given to the full-size pickup consisting of a chrome front grille with four horizontal openings, revised side and wheel-lip moldings and a change to the tailgate trim. New cloth bench seats adorned the interior, and a tilt steering wheel and cruise control were available throughout the Ram lineup.

The convertible and Shelby models, never big sellers, disappeared from the Dakota lineup, but were replaced by several new models. Chief among them was the availability throughout the Dakota lineup of the 5.2-liter V-8. Although not as potent as the Shelby version – horsepower was 165 – the addition of a V-8 in both two-wheel and four-wheel-drive Dakotas greatly increased the truck's towing capacity. The new V-8 was available only with a three-speed automatic gearbox.

To go along with the new V-8 availability, the front end received a new look and the hood was lengthened by several inches to make assembly-line installation of the V-8 easier.

At mid-year, the Club Cab was made an option on four-wheel-drive models, but was still available only with the 78 in cargo bed.

1992

A new series of Magnum engines was introduced to the full-size Ram and compact Dakota line, featuring multi-point fuel injection on both the 3.9-liter V-6 and the 5.2-liter V-8, providing dramatic increases in power. The V-6 was now rated at 180 hp, and the V-8 at 230.

A new five-speed manual transmission was now made standard, and a beefed-up four-speed automatic was optional on the V-6 while being fitted as standard on the V-8 models.

On the full-size Ram, a new dual-rear-wheel option is available on Ram 350 models, and the diesel engine was made available on the Club Cab models.

engine was made available on the Club Cab models.

Styling on the Ram and Dakota remained unchanged during this year.

1993 With word circulating among buyers that an all-new full-size pickup was due the following year, Dodge chose to make very few changes to the existing model.

The news on the Dakota front was the addition of four-wheel anti-lock brakes as an option, as well as some trim changes to the interior, including re-designed bucket seats optional on Sport models, and repositioned power-window and door-lock switches. Trim levels are redesignated as Base, Sport and SLT.

1994 This was the year that Chrysler made the move to become once again a major player in the full-size truck market. After going 22 years without any major changes, Dodge launched a completely redesigned Ram pickup, and it was an absolute stunner.

Not only was the styling distinctive, but the availability of a brawny V-10 engine vaulted Dodge into a leadership role. Sales reflected the home-run status of the new Ram: sales in 1994 soared to 232,000 – a jump of more than 140 percent.

When Dodge redesigned the Ram they opted for a big and brawny look that also was far more aerodynamic than the previous model. While Ford and Chevrolet's trucks had for years been moving

toward designs that emphasized their carlike features, Dodge built a pickup that looked like it was more akin to a semi-tractor-trailer rig than a light-duty truck. The nose retained the signature four-opening chrome grille, but the hood line was raised significantly and the front fenders were sculpted, so that they bulged. Yet flush-mounted wrap-around headlights, turn signals and side markers, combined with a heavily raked windshield and flush-mounted cab side glass gave the new Ram a very modern look.

The cargo bed was a smooth-sided design, with a slight bulge over the wheel wells. The bed was available in 78 and 96 in lengths, and cargo capacities ranged from 1,678 lb to 5,340 lb. A regular two-door cab was the only body style initially available.

The new truck was available in three load designations — 1500, 2500 and 3500, which were loosely classified as the industry standard half-ton, three-quarter-ton and one-ton payload capacities.

Engines ranged from the base 3.9-liter V-6, rated at 170 hp, to the 5.2-liter V-8 (220 hp), the 5.9-liter V-8 (230 hp), the 5.9-liter turbocharged diesel six (170 hp), and the huge 8-liter V-10, which developed 300 hp. Available transmission choices ranged from five-speed manuals to four-speed automatics; gear ratios and sturdiness vary according to the engine size.

Although very few trucks were ordered with it, the V-10 created quite a stir – in part because it was related to the 400 hp V-10 used in the Dodge Viper sports car. The pickup V-10 used a cast-iron block and cylinder heads and was of conventional overhead-valve design. It had electronic fuel injection and produced a prodigious 450 foot-pounds of torque. It had a compression ratio of 8.6-to-1 and ran on regular unleaded gasoline.

Underneath the Ram body was a chassis that was pure pickup: a ladder-type frame with a separate body. The front suspension was a torsion bar setup and out back there were conventional leaf springs. The new Ram stood tall, even in two-wheel-drive versions, adding to its overall look of toughness. Brakes were vented discs in front and drums at the rear. The rear drums came standard with an anti-lock system and the entire system had vacuum assist. A four-wheel anti-lock system was standard.

On the inside, the Ram offered a variety of features and trim levels. The base truck was called the LT, although a Work Special model, devoid of all but the most basic interior trim, was available. Next up was the ST model, with full carpeting, door trim and a split bench seat that had a large storage tray/

armrest that folded down in the center. Another handy item was a storage tray with tie-downs behind the bench seat. The top-of-the-line model was the Laramie SLT, which had cruise control, a leather-wrapped tilt steering wheel, and power windows, together with an AM-FM stereo radio with cassette player and four speakers.

Although the spotlight was very much focused on the brand new full-size Ram, a number of small but significant improvements were made to the Dakota lineup. The first and most important among them was the installation of a driver-side airbag as standard equipment. Other changes to the Dakota line-up

BELOW *This Ram 3500 Dooley is the top-dog of the Dodge lineup. Equipped with the optional eight-liter V-10, this truck has the highest towing or payload capacity in the industry.*

included revisions to the fuel-injection system on both the V-6 and V-8 engines, along with new camshafts that broadened the torque curve of both engines in addition to boosting the total torque output on the V-8 to 295 foot-pounds. Horsepower numbers are revised on both engines, with the V-6 now being rated at 175 hp and the V-8 at 220 hp. The air-conditioner used the new industry standard R-134a refrigerant, which could be used at any time without cousiing any harm to the earth's ozone layer.

the Ram and Dakota pickups. This is particularly critical in California, which in 1998 will begin enforcing much tougher emission standards. The CNG engine is rated at 200 hp.

The only other change to the Dakota was the installation of an interlock system that will allow the engine to be started only if the clutch is depressed on manual transmission pickups. This goes along with the automatic transmission interlock that required a driver to put his foot on the brake before shifting into gear. The idea behind both interlocks is to keep the car from lurching forward unexpectedly.

1996 On the full-size Ram, the 5.9-liter Cummins turbo diesel six was revised and given a significant increase in power. When combined with the five-speed manual transmission, the diesel made 215 hp; with the four-speed automatic, it was rated at just 180, owing to tuning changes necessary to ensure smooth operation with the automatic shifter. The V-10 got an improved sequential multipoint fuel-injection system that enhanced throttle response.

Other Ram changes included new optional aluminum wheels, dual lighted vanity mirrors on the Laramie SLT trim package, and the availability of a special rear-spring setup so the Ram could accommodate a camper body in the pickup bed.

The Dakota had a new, more powerful four-cylinder base engine that carried the Magnum designation. The 2.5-liter engine produced 120 hp and 145 lb-ft of torque. The new engine gave the Dakota one of the most powerful lineups in the industry. When equipped with the 5.2-liter V-8 and the optional towing package, a Dakota was rated at 2,600 lb of cargo capacity and could tow a 7,100 lb load.

1995 After all the good news over the new Ram pickup in 1994, the model continued strong into 1995 with the addition of a Club Cab body style that was available in both two- and four-wheel-drive models. The Club Cab added a full-width rear bench seat and rode on either a 138.7 in wheelbase or a 154.7 in wheelbase, depending on which cargo box is installed.

As a nod to future tightening of engine-emission standards, the 5.2-liter V-8 is offered in a version that burns compressed natural gas and is available in both

Driving the

V-10

The guy at the gas station summed up the new Dodge Ram: "Now that's a truck that looks like a truck."

In an era when trucks have become successful by looking and driving more like cars, Dodge struck a chord with the new Ram by harkening back to the days when trucks were driven by hairy-chested men.

But are those looks deceiving?

Take a spin in the top-dog Dodge pickup, a Laramie SLT equipped with the 300-hp, 8-liter V-10, and you come away with a yes and no opinion. On the outside, there is no doubt that this pickup has real guy appeal, from the power bulges to its up-high stance. For little boys who dreamed of driving big rigs but grew up to be accountants, the Ram is definitely one sexy truck.

Climb up into the cab, however, and the Ram provides enough amenities to satisfy anyone who wants to avoid the rough edges of road life. The Ram's split bench seat is very comfortable and the SLT-model cloth covering has a rich look and feel. The center fold-down storage bin is a thoughtful touch and includes room for a cellular phone, notebooks and pens and other stuff that seem to gather in pickups. The driving position is excellent, and legroom is sufficient for tall drivers. The dashboard has a full load of gauges, and the air-conditioning and radio controls are well placed and easy to reach.

This Club Cab Ram 3500 is a two-wheel-drive version of Dodge's biggest pickup. So popular was the redesigned Ram that after two years Dodge trucks had the highest resale value in the industry.

Dodge Ram

Fire up the V-10 and it comes to life with a deep rumble. Not a hot-rod rumble, but more a deep-throated, stump-pulling sound. Drop the four-speed automatic into gear and the V-10 sprints away. If you're not careful, it's easy to light up the rear tires if the cargo bed is empty.

Steering is precise, and around town the Ram handles as well as any pickup from Chevrolet or Ford. On the freeway the Dodge, with the optional 96 in bed, tends to have a bouncy ride with the cargo bed empty, due in part to the longer wheelbase and the heavy-duty rear leaf springs. Someone not accustomed to what used to be a traditional pickup ride might be disappointed. But with the bed full, or with something in tow, the handling and ride improved dramatically.

Overall, the strength of the V-10 Ram lies in the fact that it offers pickup buyers a distinct choice from what else is out there on the market. And so far buyers have responded enthusiastically, pushing resale values of the new Ram to the top of the industry.

ABOVE The Ram uses a ladder type frame with torsion bars at the front and conventional leaf springs at the back. The ride isn't the smoothest in the industry, but the Ram's road manners are still quite respectable for around-town driving.

chapter 6

The Japanese

Long before automobile manufacturers from Japan began to flood the U.S. market with their affordable, dependable, small sedans, the first inroads in the American highway from the Far East were being made in the pickup truck segment.

The first Japanese-built pickups began to appear in California as early as 1958, when Datsuns and Toyotas came off cargo ships in what was then little more than a trickle. With very short cargo beds – in some cases no more than 48 in – and cargo capacities of as little as 500 lb, these pickups had very limited uses. Farmers who grew fruit and vegetables in California's vast Central Valley found the trucks useful for maneuvering down narrow paths in their groves; the small pickups at least could carry the tools needed for pruning the trees and tending the crops. In cities such as Los Angeles the small pickups were popular with gardeners and maintenance workers who had to carry anything bulky.

The pickups had the advantage of being cheap – well under $2,000 new – reliable and easy on fuel economy. As they did with the passenger car market, the Japanese manufacturers made a long and careful study of the U.S. pickup truck market and made systematic improvements to their vehicles. Pickup beds became longer, rust-proofing was improved, engines were made larger and more powerful, and creature comforts were added.

By the 1970s, the small trucks from Toyota and Datsun (known today as Nissan) were spreading across the United States, and Detroit was forced to take notice. Like the full-sized U.S.-built pickups, the mini-pickups from Japan also began to attract customers whose primary use for a truck was not work-related. Younger buyers, priced out of some new American trucks and cars, turned to the Japanese trucks as inexpensive alternatives that by now boasted considerable style and utility.

The share of the truck market cornered by the Japanese began a steady increase, and the Big Three automakers in Detroit responded by buying mini-pickups from those Japanese automakers who had yet to make a big impact in America.

Ford was the first U.S. maker to do this with its 1972 Courier, which it bought from Mazda. At the time Ford said that these new types of pickups tended to have more appeal for younger buyers than did the traditional trucks. More than a third of all Courier buyers were under the age of 35.

Chevrolet introduced the Chevy LUV mini-pickup in 1973, a truck that it bought from Isuzu. GM simply had the Japanese manufacturer build them with the Chevrolet badge on them and put them on a U.S.-bound boat. Chrysler entered the game a little later with its 1979 D50, a four-cylinder pickup it bought from Mitsubishi.

All of imported trucks were simply stopgaps until the U.S. manufacturers could decide which way the wind was blowing and commit the hundreds of millions of dollars needed to develop their own mini pickups – something that didn't occur until the 1980s, more than 10 years after they had recognized the potential size of this market segment.

Japanese manufacturers, however, continued their relentless quest for more U.S. pickup sales and kept up a steady march to market of ever-improving vehicles. By the 1980s five major Japanese manufacturers were marketing pickups under their own names in the United States. Toyota and Nissan continued to be the two sales leaders, followed by Mazda, Mitsubishi and Isuzu. Just about the only major Japanese carmaker to shun the lucrative pickup market was Honda, much to the regret of some of its U.S. dealers.

As competition in the U.S. heated up, the Japanese builders looked for ways to keep their competitive edge. Because there was (and still is) a stiff 25 percent import tariff on trucks, Japanese manufacturers started opening plants in the United States to build pickups. Nissan was the first, opening a plant in Tennessee, and Toyota soon followed suit in Kentucky. In 1995 Toyota announced that another new plant devoted to pickups would be built in Indiana.

By the 1990s the increased competition forced some of the smaller manufacturers, notably Mazda and Isuzu, to adopt a curious game plan: they went to American manufacturers, negotiated to buy pickups from them and have them rebadged as Mazdas and Isuzus. Talk about coming full circle!

TOYOTA

In the 1990s there are two sizes of Toyota trucks in the Toyota lineup, which is unique among Japanese manufacturers. For decades, there had been just one Toyota pickup, called, simply enough, the Compact Pickup. Along the way, a few special models were called SR5, but that was just a trim and equipment upgrade on what was still the Compact Pickup. It was one of the best-selling trucks in America, and it helped Toyota create a very loyal stateside following.

In 1995, its last year of production with the Compact Pickup name, the Toyota came in both two- and four-wheel-drive models, in regular and extended cabs – the latter called Xtracab in Toyota speak – and with both a 2.4-liter four-cylinder engine and a 3-liter V-6. The inline four produced 116 hp, and had electronic fuel injection. It came with a five-speed manual transmission as standard, with the option of a

BELOW Among the Japanese manufacturers, Toyota is the No. 1 builder of pickups. This 1995 Xtracab has a V-6 engine and four-wheel-drive. To beat the yen-dollar fluctuations that have made Japanese-built trucks ever more expensive, Toyota started to build pickups in the United States.

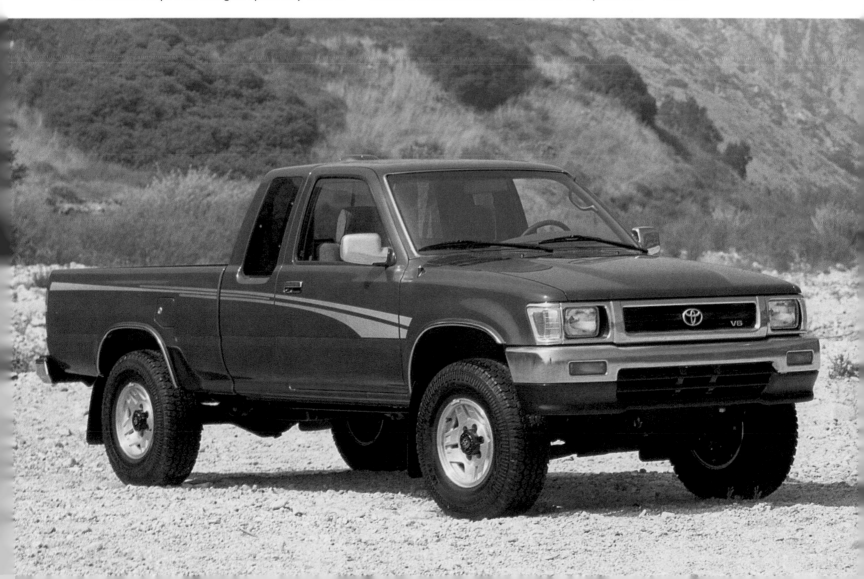

RIGHT *Toyota so far is the only manufacturer to make a stab at competing with U.S. builders in the full-size truck category. It introduced the T100, which is slightly smaller than a comparable Ford, Chevrolet, or Dodge, but sales were less than expected.*

four-speed electronically controlled automatic gearbox. Payload capacities in the 72 in cargo box of the four-cylinder pickup ranged from 1,560 to 1,800 lb on two-wheel-drive models, and from 1,815 to 2,000 lb on four-wheel-drive models, depending on equipment levels.

The V-6 produced 150 hp and also had electronic fuel injection, and it, too, was available with a four-speed automatic or a five-speed manual gearbox in both two- and four-wheel-drive configurations. Payload capacities were much the same as for the four-cylinder model. The suspension was a torsion bar setup at the front with hydraulic shock absorbers and a stabilizer bar. At the back leaf springs were used as well as hydraulic shocks. On four-wheel-drive V-6 models, gas-filled shocks replaced the liquid-filled hydraulic dampers.

Brakes were power-assisted and used vented discs at the front and drums at the rear. Rear-wheel anti-lock brakes were optional on all models and standard on the top-of-the-line SR5 V-6 trucks.

Trim levels ran from the Standard, to the DX, to the sportier SR5 model. In Standard trim, the Compact Pickup came with styled steel wheels, six inner tie-down hooks on the cargo bed, a tilt-forward bench seat, a cupholder, carpeting, a vinyl headliner and padded sun visors and arm rests. The DX package included upgraded carpeting, a better quality of cloth on the bench seat, cigarette lighter and day/night rear view mirror. On SR5 models, the V-6 came as standard equipment, as did an AM-FM

stereo radio, a 60/40 split bench seat, a passenger-visor vanity mirror, digital clock and variable-speed and intermittent windshield wipers.

The four-wheel-drive V-6 pickups came standard with a two-speed transfer case that allowed the driver to shift into four-wheel-drive at any speed up to 50 mph. The shift-on-the-move system was optional on other models. The four-wheel-drive pickups had nine inches of ground clearance and had protective skid plates under the engine, transfer case and fuel tank.

As a testament to their build quality, Toyota's Compact Pickup consistently ranked at the top of the J.D. Power Customer Satisfaction index, which measures the number of buyer complaints during the first 90 days of ownership.

In 1996, Toyota decided its restyled Compact Pickup needed a name to help identify it more readily in the marketplace. They came up with the name Tacoma, but it's unclear whether there is any relationship between the truck and the city of the same name in Washington state. Toyota says the truck's name is intended to conjure images of the rugged beauty of the Pacific Northwest.

The restyled Tacoma picked up many of the styling cues from the other Toyota pickup, the mid-sized T100. There is an overall smoothness and rounded shape to the new Tacoma that gives it a more modern, aerodynamic appeal. Like the truck it replaced, the Tacoma comes in several trim levels: the basic Tacoma, the SR5 and the new SX sport mode. The SX features bucket seats, alloy wheels, sporty stripes and graphics, and chrome bumpers.

For the first time, the four-wheel-drive version of Toyota's compact pickup gets slightly different bodywork from that of the two-wheel-drive model. The wheel arches at the front and rear have larger bulges in a styling move that Toyota hopes will suggest rugged power.

The old torsion bar front suspension was replaced by coil springs and double wishbones at each of the front corners. At the back the traditional leaf springs were retained. The steering on the Tacoma was a rack-and-pinion design with far better road feel than the recirculating ball setup on previous models. On the brakes, Toyota made a full four-wheel anti-lock system an option.

Under the hood, more power was added. The base 2.4-liter inline four was topped with double overhead camshafts, which boosted power by 26 to 142 hp. A new 2.7-liter inline four was added and made the base engine in 4 x 4 models. The new four put out 150 horsepower and a substantial 177 foot-pounds of torque. King of the new Tacoma engine lineup was a 3.4-liter V-6 that replaced the old 3-liter unit and produced 190 hp and a whopping 220 foot-pounds of torque. The new V-6 increased the Tacoma's towing capacity to 5,000 lb.

Transmissions were upgraded for the new Tacoma. The five-speed manual had a smoother-shifting linkage, and the electronically controlled four-speed automatic made a better job of quickly finding the right gear for each driving condition. The shift-on-the-move four-wheel-drive system was now activated by a dash-mounted push-button switch.

Inside, there was more room in the Tacoma than in previous Compact Pickups, and on Xtracab models the flip-down jump seats had a center table. For the first time, a driver's-side airbag was installed in a Toyota pickup.

The Tacoma and its predecessors have proven very popular with buyers, but the same can't be said of the T100 pickup that Toyota introduced in 1992. Until the arrival of the T100, none of the Japanese pickups could be seen as legitimate challengers to the full-size pickups that were the bread-and-butter models at Ford, Chevrolet and Dodge. The T100 proved something of a disappointment.

It wasn't a full-size truck, but rather a mid-size model akin to Dodge's Dakota. There was no V-8 on the option list, and the 3.4-liter V-6 was not brawny enough with just 150 hp. To make matters worse, the T100 had bland styling.

Buyers of full-size trucks stayed away in droves, and traditional consumers of compact pickups didn't see any added advantages to the T100 to justify its steep list price. Because it was built in Japan, the T100 was subject to the 25 percent import tariff, and it was introduced at a time when the dollar was weak against the yen, further driving up the T100's price. A well equipped T100 would sticker at $25,000 or more. Toyota dealers accustomed to having pickups fly off their lots were faced with hundreds of T100s sitting there gathering dust.

This is not to say the T100 was a bad truck. The fit and finish were among the best, and those who did buy T100s found that they had the same utter reliability as the Compact Pickups. The 96 in. bed could carry most items, although overall cargo capacity was limited to a maximum of 2,480 lb.

Starting in 1995, Toyota made a concerted effort to deal with some of the criticisms leveled at the T100. First, it added an Xtracab version, appealing to a segment of the full-size market that has been the fastest-growing. The Xtracab offered 21.4 cu. ft. of interior room, and the rear bench seat was among the most comfortable in the extended-cab field. The look of the truck was helped in the Xtracab by the addition of the two side windows and the shortening of the pickup bed by more than 18 in. (One of the criticisms of the regular cab T100 was that the front was too small in proportion to the cargo bed).

Next, Toyota addressed the power issue by offering a 190 hp 3.4-liter V-6 that pushed the T100 near the top of the class among six-cylinder pickups. A 2.7-liter 150 hp four was now the standard engine. A five-speed manual or four-speed automatic transmission was available, as was four-wheel-drive.

The last – and maybe most critical area – price, would be harder to fix, since it is subject in part to the whims of the international monetary market and political breezes in Washington. As a move in the right direction, Toyota announced in 1995 that it would build a new factory in Indiana to build T100 pickups as a way of lowering its price in America.

Driving the

The first thing you notice about the T100 4 x 4 extended cab from Toyota is that it's a very big truck. Not as big, perhaps, as a full-size Ford, Chevy or Dodge. But by anyone's standard this is a big, brawny vehicle.

You climb up into the cabin, which is quite roomy and well appointed. The seats are covered in a rich gray fabric, and the fold-down armrest has plenty of storage space inside. The seating position is high and all-around visibility is very good. There's a full pod of gauges, and the optional compact disc player/AM/FM stereo radio has a quality sound to it.

Fire up the 3.4-liter V-6 and its 190 horses roar to life. Slip the automatic transmission into gear, and a tap on the gas pedal shows that the engine's power is available from very low revolutions. Stand on the gas and the T100 sprints to 60 mph in under 9 seconds with just the rear wheels engaged. It's a good 2 seconds slower in 4 x 4 mode, but few people use that setup in everyday street driving.

BELOW *Driving the T-100 is a satisfying experience. The legendary Toyota fit and finish are apparent, and the 190-horsepower V-6 delivers plenty of power. The truck's towing capacity is rated at 5,500 pounds.*

Steering is very precise and the T100 handles curves better than you would expect in a 4 x 4 that has nine inches of ground clearance. It goes where you point it, and the front disc/rear drum brakes inspire confidence.

On the highway the T100 rides very smoothly and, except for the high-up view of the road, it would be very easy to forget you are driving a Toyota pick-up. Yet with several hundred pounds of tools in the pickup bed and a tandem axle trailer with a race car on board hitched behind the T100, it pulled willingly. It tended to run out of steam at speeds over 70 mph when fully loaded, but away from a stoplight the V-6 had plenty of low-end grunt — dispelling one of the criticisms of the T100: its lack of a V-8.

So what's wrong with this truck — and why doesn't it sell better?

First is the price. As nice a truck as it is, a T100 with all the goodies will sticker close to $30,000. That's several thousand dollars more than a fully

T-100

loaded Dodge Ram or Ford F150. Knock the T100's price back to about $22,000 fully loaded, and they would zip out the door.

Another problem is that there are just a heck of a lot of good trucks out there on the market, and the only thing to give the T100 an edge over another, larger truck is that it's made by Toyota and it should have the famous Toyota reliability. That's a selling point – but nowadays the trucks from Ford, Chevy and Dodge are also very reliable.

Lastly, a factor that perhaps no one wants to admit is that there is a certain amount of chauvinism among buyers of big pickups. Many of them believe that the full-size pickup is the last bastion of American craftsmanship in the automobile marketplace and they just aren't interested in a big pickup from Japan.

ABOVE *Although it has a 190-horsepower V-6, the T-100 gives up ground to U.S. pickups because it lacks a V-8. This 1995 four-wheel-drive SR5 model is a rugged performer with better-than-average quality ratings.*

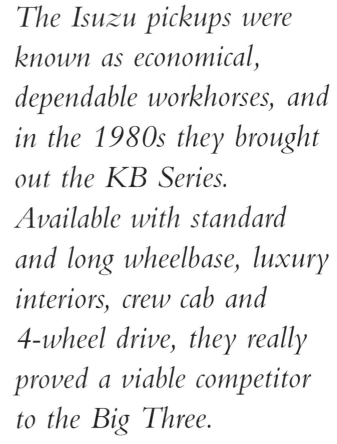

The Isuzu pickups were known as economical, dependable workhorses, and in the 1980s they brought out the KB Series. Available with standard and long wheelbase, luxury interiors, crew cab and 4-wheel drive, they really proved a viable competitor to the Big Three.

NISSAN

ABOVE *Smooth-sided cargo beds and a stylish chrome grille were some of the new features for 1995 on this V-6-powered 4X4 SE pickup. Nissan is the No. 2 Japanese pickup builder in the United States.*

Of the Japanese manufacturers, Nissan traditionally has offered the widest range of equipment and trim levels on its pickups — though they are all based on one size of truck. Its 1995 lineup was typical of what Nissan has historically offered in both two-wheel-drive and four-wheel-drive pickups. There were five versions of the truck in two-wheel-drive configuration and four 4 x 4 versions.

The base pickup came with a 134 hp, 2.4-liter single-overhead-camshaft inline four that had sequential multi-point fuel injection. In a nod to multivalve technology, the base engine has three valves per cylinder for better breathing at higher rpm. Next up the option scale was a 3.4-liter V-6 that had only two valves per cylinder but produced 153 hp. Both engines could be ordered with five-speed manual or four-speed automatic transmissions.

The body on the pickup could be had as a standard two-door, a King Cab extended cab version with a back seat, or a long-bed version that increased

the length of the cargo box from 72 to 90 in. And there were two trim levels – the standard and the XE, which included such upgrades as carpeting, bucket seats and other comfort and appearance enhancements.

So the five two-wheel-drive models were the standard four-cylinder, the XE with the four, the King Cab with the four or the V-6, and the Long Bed V6. In the 4 x 4 arena, all of the two-wheel-drive models except the base standard truck were available. The flagship Nissan pickup was the 4 x 4 SE V-6 King Cab, which came equipped with air-conditioning, all-terrain tires, fender flares, a six-way adjustable driver's seat, fold-down rear jump seats, cruise control, tilt steering wheel, a 100-watt AM-FM cassette stereo, sliding rear window, and, finally, a chrome rear step-bumper.

As wide-ranging as Nissan's lineup was, by 1995 the company was having trouble keeping up, in part because of the intense competition posed by industry leaders Ford Ranger and Chevrolet S10, which between them sold more than 700,000 units. Toyota sold more than 220,000 compact trucks, while Nissan struggled along at about 112,000 in pickup sales – almost half.

To help pare costs and simplify its lineup, starting with its 1996 models Nissan took a more one-size-fits-all approach. It vanquished the V-6 from the lineup – leaving just the 2.4-liter four – and reduced the basic models it offers from nine to four: the standard and King Cab body styles, available in two or four-wheel-drive versions. Whether that strategy will see Nissan through the 1990s until it can bring an all-new pickup to market is debatable.

ABOVE *When the first Nissan-built truck came to the U.S. shores, it was called a Datsun and it was built in Japan. This 1995 Nissan two-wheel drive XE pickup was built at a Nissan factory in Tennessee.*

MAZDA

Over the years, Mazda has brought a lot of interesting and reliable pickups to the United States, including several models that used the Wankel rotary engine that Mazda helped perfect and still uses in its RX7 sports car. Since 1971 more than 1 million Mazda pickups have been sold in America, and according to the company more than 90 percent of those trucks are still on the road.

But as the truck market has become more crowded – and as the company has suffered through several years of declining passenger-car sales – Mazda has done what U.S. manufacturers did more than two years ago. In search of a compact pickup for the U.S. market, Mazda went to Ford at the start of the 1994 model year and commissioned the No. 1 U.S. truck maker to build Mazda pickups using the very successful Ford Ranger as a base.

That move should come as no surprise. Ford owns a 25 percent stake in Mazda, and it was Mazda that provided Ford's first compact pickup, the Courier. It made excellent sense to clone the most successful compact pickup in the U.S. market, the Ford Ranger.

Mazda and Ford share a few other cars and trucks, including the Mazda MX-6/Ford Probe and the two-door Ford Explorer/Mazda Navajo. For the Mazda B-series pickup, the Ranger is reskinned with a different grille and slightly different side sheetmetal, and it is produced at a Ford plant in Edison, N.J.

Whether this is a long-range strategy for Mazda or, like the Ford, Chevrolet and Dodge operation of the 1970s, is a stop-gap measure until a new pickup can be developed is still unclear. While Mazda makes its own pickups for the Japanese market, company officials feel these could not compete in the U.S. now because of international currency fluctuations and U.S.-imposed import taxes.

Because it is a reskinned Ranger, the Mazda B-series is available in a wide variety of configurations. The series is divided into three numerical designations depending on engine size. The base B2300 uses a 2.3-liter inline four that produces 112 hp. The B3000 uses a 145 hp, 3.4-liter V-6, while the B4000 offers a 160-hp 4-liter V-6.

The body comes in both standard cab and an extended cab called Cab Plus, and there are three trim levels – base, SE and LE. The SE is more sport-oriented and the LE has more luxury touches. There also are two bed lengths – 78 and 96 in. – and all models are available in two- or four-wheel-drive. The latter uses Ford's shift-on-the-fly push-button selector to go between two- and four-wheel-drive at any speed. A five-speed manual or a four-speed automatic transmission option is available on all models.

For 1996, Mazda's B-series shares with Ford the distinction of being the only pickup to offer a passenger-side airbag that has an on-off switch to allow a child safety seat to be mounted on the passenger side. Other safety features include a driver-side airbag, full anti-lock brakes and side door beams.

ISUZU

The other Japanese manufacturer to take the path of least cost toward offering U.S. buyers a pickup is Isuzu. Although it is primarily a truck builder in Japan – and now no longer offers a passenger car for sale in the United States – when it was time to replace the aging P'up, as its pickup was known, Isuzu turned to General Motors, which now owns a share of the company.

What the two came up with was a new truck called the Hombre, which has Isuzu designed sheet metal – grille, hood, front fenders and body side panels – wrapped around the chassis and bed of the Chevrolet S10 pickup. Unlike Mazda, which negotiated for a full-range of trucks with Ford, Isuzu opted to build only one model.

The Hombre came as a two-wheel-drive pickup with a standard two-door cab and a 78 in cargo bed. A driver-side airbag was standard. Power was from the Chevy 2.2-liter inline four, which put out 118 hp. A five-speed manual transmission was standard and a four-speed automatic was available. Even the option list was shortened to include just air-conditioning, a 60/40 split bench seat, AM/FM stereo radio with cassette player, and a sliding rear glass window.

The benefit of all this paring down was that even fully loaded an Isuzu Hombre had a sticker price of

BELOW *In Japan, Isuzu is primarily known as a truck builder, although the company also makes passenger cars. In the United States, after trying to compete with a full line of cars and trucks, Isuzu has pulled back to just trucks and sport utility vehicles. This 1978 Isuzu pickup followed the company philosophy of just offering a solid work truck.*

about $14,000, which might have made it attractive —
until buyers realized that Chevrolet could sell them
virtually the same truck for hundreds of dollars less.
(Isuzu has to tack on some profit over what it paid
Chevy for the trucks.)

Nonetheless, this is a game that Isuzu under-
stands well. It sold its Rodeo sport utility vehicle to
Honda, which renamed it Passport, and its Trooper
to Honda's upscale Acura division, which renamed it
SLX and passed it off as a luxury sport utility vehicle
to compete with Range Rover.

The world of trucks is no longer a simple place.

MITSUBISHI

The other Japanese manufacturer to take a bare-
bones approach to offering a pickup in the U.S.
market is Mitsubishi. Unlike Mazda and Isuzu, however, Mitsubishi offers a truck that it designs and
builds in Japan. This is odd: Mitsubishi has had a very
close relationship with Chrysler and almost certainly
could have rebadged a Dakota pickup and passed it
off as one of its own.

The Mitsubishi pickup, called the Mighty Max, at
one time was available in a variety of trims and
drivetrain configurations. By 1996, however, it had
shrunk to just one model aimed at first-time or
entry-level pickup buyers.

The two-wheel-drive Mighty Max had a 2.4-liter
inline four that produced 116 hp. The engine used
electronic fuel injection, roller rocker arms and dual
balance shafts to make it one of the smoothest fours
on the market.

A five-speed manual transmission was standard
and a four-speed automatic was optional; the brakes
were front discs and rear drums. Mitsubishi claimed
that the rear drums automatically adjusted line
pressure to compensate for various load levels in the
72 in cargo bed. The maximum payload capacity was
1,585 lb.

Like the Isuzu, the Mighty Max had a very limited
option list: air-conditioning, AM/FM stereo radio with
cassette, a single-disc compact disc player, a chrome
rear bumper, body side moldings and power steering.

*OPPOSITE This
Mitsubishi Mighty Max pickup
represents a single-model
approach to the U.S. market.
The Mighty Max is available
only as a two-wheel-drive, and
a limited number of options are
offered as a way of keeping the
price down.*

chapter 7

It's a given of the automobile world that if two people have a conveyance with wheels, it will only be a matter of time before some- one organizes a race. In the case of the pickup truck, it took about 70 years before it became a serious competition vehicle.

Although primarily designed as a work vehicle, the pickup has been well suited to several forms of competition, and fans have responded by turning out in huge numbers. One of the axioms of automobile racing, particularly the NASCAR oval track events, is that fan appreciation is related in part to the fact that they can identify with the production-based cars that are on the track. With the pickup, perhaps, that is even more the case because of the burgeoning numbers on the road and the obvious truth that a pickup is often more affordable than other racing vehicles, for example, a Ford Thunderbird.

Truck competitions fall into three or four different categories, at least one of which can barely be called racing in the classic sense. The big break for

pickups as glamor—competition vehicles came in the form of what are now called Monster Truck ex- hibitions. The phenomenon began in the 1970s, and these trucks are pickups on steroids, with huge tires and massive suspensions that push the pickup body 10 to 20 feet above the ground. The favorite form of Monster Truck competition involves using the trucks to crush cars.

At about the same time, off-road racing started to become a very popular sport. The best-known of these races is the Baja 1000, the unforgiving test of men and machines that runs the length of the Baja California peninsula in northwest Mexico. All sorts of vehicles including cars, sport-utility vehicles and motorcycles compete in that event, but the pickups are always the stars of the race.

Stadium racing is derivative of off-road events in which some of the types of obstacles that are regu- larly encountered in the Baja race, for example, are recreated inside sports stadiums, and trucks (as well as motorcycles in their own class) then race around this set course.

But as popular as these events are, the wide- spread acceptance of the pickup as an object of speed would appear to be as a result of NASCAR's creation of the SuperTruck racing series.

NASCAR is the sanctioning body of American stock-car racing, the most popular form of auto- mobile racing in the world, based on attendance and television viewership. Starting in 1995, NASCAR

BELOW *The Monster Truck theme is definitely an American institution. Only big Detroit iron need apply.*

expanded its racing series to encompass trucks, holding 20 races at tracks across the United States.

All of these forms of competition have added prestige and glamor to the pickup, so much so that manufacturers are always very quick to use these events as sales tools.

Success in off-road racing confers an aura of toughness; a win in SuperTruck implies speed and agility. As for the Monster Trucks — well, put one on a dealer's lot and the kids will drag mom and dad to see it, giving the dealer a chance to sell the family a new pickup.

Here's a look at the major forms of pickup truck competition:

MONSTER TRUCKS

It's hard to point to a single person and say that they were the creator of a competition series, but arguably that's what can be done when it comes to Monster Trucks.

Bob Chandler of St. Louis, MO., is the father of the Monster Truck. In the mid 1970s, when virtually everyone used their pickup as a work vehicle, Chandler was no different. He was a construction contractor and he used his Ford F250 four-wheel-drive pickup to haul building supplies and to pick its

way through muddy construction sites. Weekends he would take his family camping or fishing, using his truck's four-wheel-drive capabilities to reach very out-of-the-way sites.

In the course of logging all these tough miles, he would break things on his truck. Chandler became frustrated at what he saw as a lack of really heavy-duty parts for his 4 x 4. Being something of a back-yard inventor, he began to make his own replacement parts, and started beefing up his truck. He looked at all the other 4 x 4 pickups out there and recognized an untapped market for what he was doing to his own truck.

Striking out in what was then a business wilderness, Chandler and his wife Marilyn quit the construction business and opened their own company, called Midwest Four Wheel Drive. And the family 4 x 4 became a promotional tool. Chandler kept (quite literally) building up the truck, adding new suspension and chassis parts that allowed him to install larger and larger tires. Eventually, the Ford pickup body was sitting on a four-wheel-drive chassis that had 66 in tires taken from a farm-manure spreader. It was called Bigfoot, named after the mythical hairy beast said to inhabit the deep forests of North America.

ABOVE *It's a singularly American form of motorsport: Bigfoot, the original monster truck, flies off a ramp and prepares to crush a line of junk cars.*

The truck became an attraction in itself, and in 1978 appeared in its first car show in Denver. It also had a cameo movie appearance in *Take This Job and Shove It* in 1979. But the real popularity of Bigfoot and other trucks like it took off after an appearance in 1982 in the Silverdome stadium in Pontiac, MI.

The U.S. auto industry was then in one of its worst slumps, and the 72,000 people who were in the Silverdome that night cheered wildly when Bigfoot, as part of its show, reared up and crushed a line of Japanese automobiles. Since then, car crushing has become a regular part of Monster Truck performances. And the events have gone beyond car-crushing to include timed races through obstacle courses, pulling contests and mud-bog races. The

allure of the Monster Trucks seems to somewhat mirror the popularity of pickups in general: these are vehicles that people love to see get dirty.

Annually, as many as 15 million people attend shows featuring Monster Truck events, and these distinctly American vehicles have toured the world.

So what goes into a 10,000-pound pickup that can run up a ramp, fly 30 feet in the air and come crashing down without damage? A lot of leading-edge automotive technology – that's what.

The engine on one of Chandler's latest Bigfoot pickups is a 572 cu. in. V-8 that is supercharged, runs on methanol fuel and produces 1,600 hp at 7300 rpm. The transmission is a highly modified Ford C6 three-speed automatic, which drives both axles using a

BELOW Standing 20-feet tall, Bigfoot has a tube frame, a composite body, and an engine that rides amidships. There is a four-speed automatic that powers two transfer cases.

four-speed transfer case, special driveshafts and ZF limited-slip differentials on both axles.

All of this is mounted in a tube-frame chassis computer-designed to provide maximum suspension travel when the 10,000-pound truck comes to ground after a ramp jump. One major departure from the production pickups is that in the Bigfoot trucks the engine is mounted amidships, behind the driver's seat, for better weight distribution.

The body on a Monster Truck may look stock, but don't be fooled. Like race cars, the Monster Truck bodies are fiberglass or carbon-fiber shells that have the same shape as the production vehicle, but are lighter and can easily be replaced in the event that there is a crash.

An interesting side-effect is that as the Monster Trucks grew in popularity in the 1980s, people began to modify their street trucks to resemble pickups like Bigfoot. The only problem was that these trucks stood so high off the ground that they were susceptible to tipping over in extreme conditions, and a few reckless owners crushed cars in parking lots when trying to impress their buddies. As a result a number of state motor-vehicle laws were changed to outlaw the wildest Monster Trucks from the road by setting maximum bumper heights and dictating that the fenders on a truck had to cover a certain percentage of the tires.

Despite these on-the-road restrictions, Monster Trucks remain a wildly popular offshoot of the pickup culture.

ABOVE Here is where it all started. Two Bigfoot monster trucks nearly dwarf the home of Bigfoot 4X4 Inc., a parts supply house and promotions company founded in St. Louis, MO.

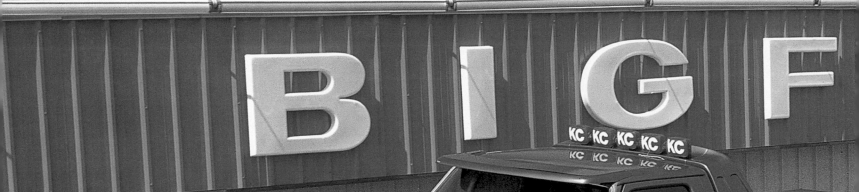

SPECIFICATIONS OF A MONSTER TRUCK

Bigfoot XI

BODY: *1993 Ford F-250*

CHASSIS: *Custom tube frame with roll cage*

ENGINE: *572 cu. in. Ford block with supercharger*

FUEL: *Methanol*

HORSEPOWER: *1,610 @ 7300 rpm*

TRANSMISSION: *Ford C6, three-speed automatic*

SUSPENSION: *Four-link, front and rear*

TIRES: *Firestone 66x43x25 Floatation*

HEIGHT: *10 ft*

WIDTH: *11 ft 9 in*

WEIGHT: *10,000 lb*

ABOVE *A Toyota unlimited off-road racing pickup pounds over desert terrain. In the top class, the trucks have lightweight body shells and special tube frames to help weather the abuse.*

OFF-ROAD RACING

If there ever was a form of auto racing that could truly be called a grass-roots effort, it must be the Baja 1000. Adventuresome drivers and motorcycle riders from California would, on their own, start out at the northern end of the Baja peninsula outside the town of Tijuana, a few miles south of San Diego, and run as fast as they could across rugged country to La Paz, in the far south of the peninsula – a trip of about 1,000 miles in total.

Most of the early racers' exploits were the stuff of campfire tales and garage talk – there were no official records. The first to record an official time for the run were two motorcycle riders, Dave Elkins and Bill Robertson Jr., who in 1962 made the trip in 39 hours 54 minutes. Their method of proving the validity of their claim was crude. They started at the telegraph office in Tijuana and had a sheet of paper time-stamped there. When they rode into La Paz, they went to that town's telegraph office and had the same sheet of paper stamped. There were no trophies, no prize money, no other competitors, even. Just the bragging rights.

The Baja run might have continued in relative obscurity if it had not been for an effort by Chevrolet to prove the toughness of their pickups. Shortly after the Elkins and Robertson run, Chevrolet went to race-car builder Bill Stroppe in Long Beach, CA, and commissioned him to equip a small fleet of Chevrolet pickups for an off-road run to La Paz. Although no time was kept on the run, all the Chevrolet trucks made it to La Paz, and Chevy's advertising department made a very big deal out of the accomplishment.

Various other singular efforts to run the Baja were held between 1963 and 1967, with motorcycles, special dune buggies designed for the event, standard passenger cars and pickup trucks.

The event that is today known as the Baja 1000 dates from 1967, when a group called the National Off-Road Racing Association sponsored the first organized run with 68 entries. The run that year was from Tijuana to La Paz, although the first 50-odd miles of the event – from Tijuana to the port city of Ensenada – was run on normal roads at near legal speeds. The winner that year was a motorcycle rider.

The next year the race start was moved south to Ensenada, where the no-holds-barred competition began. Over the years, the course has changed from a straight run to La Paz to a circuit that began and ended in Ensenada, to an alternate circuit that started and ended in Mexicali, on the national frontier some 95 miles east of Tijuana.

The race has had political problems: in 1973 the Mexican government revoked the permit it had given the U.S.-based NORRA and turned the race over to some local Mexican businessmen. That was a disaster, and in 1974 there was no race. In 1975, the Mexican government invited a U.S. group called SCORE (Short Course Off-Road Enthusiasts) to organize the event, and SCORE has been doing so ever since.

Over the years, the event has become an advertising bonanza for pickup manufacturers who want buyers to know their trucks are tough. Walker Evans is the Nigel Mansell of the Baja 1000, and in 1979 he posted an overall win in a pickup – a tough

B E L O W *The off-road racing craze started with the Baja 1000 run in the 1960s. The idea at first was to simply go from Tijuana to La Paz as fast as possible. In later years, a specific course with checkpoints was used.*

feat given that the motorcycles and dune buggies are in most respects better suited to the terrain.

A number of other off-road races in the scrub and desert regions of the American Southwest were created by SCORE, with the Baja race the crown jewel, much like the Indianapolis 500. The people who drive these races endure hour upon hour of punishment to their bodies, and it's often a case of which will break first – the crew or the vehicle.

Pickup trucks that compete in these events fall into several different classes. The premier class is called Trophy Truck. These vehicles are tube-framed, purpose-built racing vehicles. They have custom suspensions designed to soak up the punishment these trucks take when they go pounding across sage and sand dunes at speeds above 100 mph in some sections. They can have one or two seats, and the

rules and regulations are very loose regarding engines and transmissions.

The only firm rule is that they must in general have the same appearance as the production truck that carries the same name. To accomplish that, fiberglass panels are fashioned in the overall shape of a showroom vehicle and then draped over the steel-tube frame. In reality, very few of the trucks in this class are even close to production vehicles in terms of weight and overall dimensions.

Another group, closer to production vehicles, is Class 4, which is for production-based long-wheel-base pickups and sport-utility vehicles. There is a stipulation that pickups that race in this class must have two seats, and there are limits to the modifications that can be made to the suspension travel.

Class 7 encompasses production mini and mid-

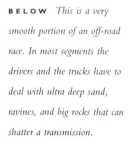

BELOW This is a very smooth portion of an off-road race. In most segments the drivers and the trucks have to deal with ultra deep sand, ravines, and big rocks that can shatter a transmission.

size pickups, both two-wheel-drive and four-wheel-drive. Pickups in this category must have a wheelbase no longer than 125 in. Entrants are permitted to make a wide range of modifications to the trucks, and engines as large as 4.5-liters can be used.

A subcategory, Class 7S, is for the same pickups but with very few modifications from stock allowed, and engine size is limited to no larger than 3 liters.

Class 8 is for two-wheel-drive full-size American-made pickups, with no restrictions on engine size except, for example, that a Ford pickup must have a Ford engine that is available as a normal option.

There are also categories for absolutely stock mini and full-size pickups.

Manufacturers from the United States and Japan spend millions of dollars fielding teams for these events, which draw hundreds of competitors. A typical effort to win the Baja race involves months of preparation, pre-running the route you think the course will take, and setting up a fleet of support vehicles to meet you at checkpoints to make the inevitable repairs. It's not unusual for steering boxes to be shattered on rocks, for suspensions to bend and break several times, and for tires and wheels to be destroyed.

It's a tough form of racing that takes the true measure of a driver and a pickup.

ABOVE A Toyota takes a fast turn on a rocky stretch of desert. It's not unusual for major repairs to be made to vehicles during the Baja 1000.

Sponsors know a crowd-pleaser when they see one, and the Nascar SuperTruck series had no trouble getting corporations to sign on. Everything from law care products to batteries to brake pads were advertised across the flanks of the race trucks. Paint schemes also were designed so that the trucks looked like 160-mph versions of their product packages.

ABOVE *When they aren't being raced, pickups are frequently seen at race tracks as pace vehicles or emergency vehicles, like this Ford F-150.*

RUCK OF THE FORD 200 SUPERTRUCK RACE BY FORD CREDIT

STADIUM RACING

Popular as an advertising gimmick as the Baja 1000 is, it has never been much of a spectator race. Each year a few thousand hearty souls brave the desert heat, the rugged terrain and the added excitement of rattlesnakes in the brush to catch glimpses of motorcycles, buggies and trucks flying through the air or throwing up a rooster tail of sand.

Nonetheless, race organizers believed the interest was there for a spectator event — if only the desert could be brought to the paying customer. Baja 1000 organizer SCORE was formed in 1973 to meet that need.

It's founder was racer and promoter Mickey Thompson, who always pushed the envelope, whether it was in drag racing with his multiple-engine machines, or at Indianapolis with his four-wheel-drive racers. He arranged for a five-mile desert course to be laid out around the famed Riverside Raceway, south of San Bernardino, CA, and invited the public to come and watch the same people who had made the Baja 1000 famous compete on a shorter track.

Thousands of people showed up to watch that first event, and it became a fixture on the southern California racing scene, at times out-drawing the Indycar races at the nearby Ontario Speedway. But it soon became apparent that the facilities at Riverside were becoming doomed by encroaching residential development, and new venues were needed.

In the early 1980s Thompson and others hit on the idea of creating small, portable tracks that could be set up inside football stadiums around the country. The regular playing field would be covered over, and then dump trucks would bring in dirt and bulldozers would shape the earth into a race track with berms and jumps and other types of hazards.

Fans could see all the action from the comfort of a stadium seat and, in huge domed venues like the Astrodome in Houston, TX, racegoers wouldn't even have to worry about the weather.

It was an amazingly astute move. Off-road racing became known as stadium racing, and a new racing venue was created that could bring the sport to parts of the country where it could never have been staged before. Promoters packaged the races with thrill shows, tractor pulls, Monster Truck exhibitions, and tens of thousands of people filled the stadiums to

hear the noise and see the action. Manufacturers were pleased because it gave them a chance to showcase their pickups to even larger audiences.

In relation to the stock pickups, the stadium trucks are more akin to the Trophy Trucks in the Baja 1000, though on a more limited scale. Like the Trophy Trucks, they generally start with a custom race-bred steel-tube frame, and then production items like engines and transmissions are installed. Suspensions are usually custom built and the trucks are set up to be more nimble than the Baja racers. Fiberglass or carbon-fiber bodywork that more closely resembles the production pickup is hung on the tube frame.

The pickups used in these stadium races tend to be the mini or mid-size pickups because the tracks are very short — a third of a mile, usually — and are very tight, with turns that double back on each other to fit within the stadium. Engine modifications are more restrictive than in true off-road races, in part to keep costs down, but also because high-horsepower engines are not essential to winning. Top speeds are generally under 60 mph, so the key to a fast truck is one that corners well and can accelerate quickly.

As with the Baja 1000, toughness is a necessary feature of stadium trucks. The racing is very competitive, and the tracks are narrow. So fender-benders are common, and it's not unusual for a pickup to get rolled on its side, or upended completely — and then to get straightened out and continue in the race.

All the major manufacturers — Ford, Chevrolet, Dodge, Toyota and Nissan — are represented in the stadium racing series.

SUPERTRUCK

Although fun and hugely popular as they have become over the past 20 years, Monster Truck, Baja 1000 and stadium racing were hardly seen as real racing by some pickup fans. Trucks that go flying through the air, crush Japanese cars, or throw up some desert sand may be fun, but real racing involved going fast on pavement, and running door-handle to door-handle into a turn. Only a car can do that really well, surely?

Well, NASCAR, for one, seriously disagrees that real racing is limited to cars. NASCAR, the organization that sanctions the wildly popular Winston Cup stock car series, in 1994 began a new series in which the race cars would be based on trucks.

Called the SuperTruck series, the new form of racing is designed to appeal to fans who know that trucks aren't just for hauling any more. Manufacturers know the value of having a racing image, especially NASCAR. Since the 1950s, the Big Three in Detroit have followed the adage that says if you win on Sunday, you sell on Monday. If fans see a Chevrolet Monte Carlo in Victory Lane at Daytona, there will be a halo effect that carries over to the more mundane Monte Carlo for sale at Chevy dealer showrooms across the country.

It is a winning formula that has kept manufacturers pouring millions of dollars a year into NASCAR teams, and kept tens of millions of fans tuning in to race telecasts. So when NASCAR came up with the SuperTruck series, it seemed a natural. Pickup buyers are an extremely loyal bunch, and they would likely root wildly for the Ford F150 on the track that looks a lot like the F150 the fan will drive home from the races.

With more than a year under its belt, the SuperTruck series appeared to be a huge success. Almost all the events were sellouts, and the competition — like that of the first-rank stock cars — was intense. Mike Skinner, driving a Chevrolet C1500 pickup, won the first event at Phoenix by just 0.09 of a second! All 20 events in 1995 were televised nationally, and Skinner went on to win the first championship.

In construction and specifications, there is scant difference between a SuperTruck and one of the cars in the Busch Grand National series — which is considered the next step down from the premier Winston Cup series. The truck starts with a tube-frame chassis from which all the suspension parts are hung. The front suspension uses unequal-length A-arms, with coil springs over gas-filled shock absorbers. The rear suspension is a solid differential with coil springs and shocks.

A SuperTruck chassis has a 112 in wheelbase and is two inches longer and nine inches taller than a NASCAR stock car — although overall it weighs a bit less than the 2,800 lb Winston Cup car. The cockpit of a SuperTruck is shorter — front to back — than a Winston Cup car, but is enclosed in the same type of safety roll cage as on the race cars.

A SuperTruck is a single-seat machine and, because of the shorter cockpit dimensions, the driver tends to sit more upright than he would in a stock car, and the steering wheel is closer to the driver's body. Engines for the V-8-powered SuperTrucks are of 358 cu. in. and are limited to a cylinder-head compression ratio of 9.5-to-1. Horsepower is rated at about 700, and that power is delivered to the rear wheels through a four-speed manual transmission.

The series is limited to body styles of the three American full-size pickups: The Chevrolet/GMC C1500, the Ford F150 and the Dodge 1500. The SuperTrucks sit considerably lower than their street counterparts, but otherwise the dimensions and shape are nearly identical.

Each race shop is provided with a set of body shape templates by NASCAR that are identical to the templates used at the track to check the legality of each race truck. The templates conform almost exactly to the shape of the production pickup of an inch.

The hood and roof of a SuperTruck must be stock parts that come from the manufacturer, while the nose and tail are removable carbon fiber shells sold specifically for the race trucks. The side panels and other body parts are fabricated by each shop and welded to the chassis. Under the rear where the pickup bed would be on a production truck, Super Truck teams locate fuel pumps, gas lines and the fuel tank. At the end of the pickup bed is an air spoiler that helps keep the rear end glued to the track at high speed.

Because of the $3 million in prize money put up for the first year, the SuperTruck series drew full 28-car fields. Although the series attracted new drivers from other types of racing — sports cars, dirt tracks, and open-wheeled cars — a number of big-name NASCAR stars became involved. Some of them were truck owners, while others, like Terry Labonte, showed up behind the wheel themselves at some of the races.

So how different is it to drive a SuperTruck from a regular NASCAR stocker? Butch Gilliland, who has driven in Winston Cup, lapped the short track at Tucson, AZ, in a SuperTruck in a time within a tenth of a second of his best Winston Cup effort there. Says Mike Bliss, a full-time competitor in the series: "It has been tough trying to remember to call it a race 'truck' rather than a race car."

BELOW Although they look like pickups, the race trucks are really NASCAR stock car frames with pickup body shells draped over them.

Not since the true hot rods of the 1940s and 1950s has there been a vehicle so ripe for customization as the pickup truck. When pickups first came on the scene some 80 years ago, a custom pickup meant one that had a tow hook attached to make it a tow truck.

Today, custom means wild and pretty – from fancy side stripes to eye-popping colors to fender flairs, fog lights, spoilers and beyond, to just about anything the mind can imagine. A significant number of pickup buyers – perhaps as many as 20 percent – see their new trucks as blank canvases on which they can create.

The trend to custom trucks started with the darling of the young buyers in the 1970s, the Japanese pickups. Cheap and easy to work on, these pickups fell into the hands of kids who a decade earlier would have been customizing '57 Chevys. In California –

from where all automotive trends seem to come – it was not uncommon to see a Datsun pickup that had been lowered to within a few inches of the ground, had chrome wheels with fat low-profile tires sticking out beyond the fender wells and a chrome exhaust pipe poking out the back. The body would be painted chartreuse or chrome yellow, and it might have contrasting swirls painted down the side. Some trucks had panoramas painted on the tailgate. There were sunroofs – or no roofs – on many pickups, and the bed might have a camper shell covering it with stereo gear underneath.

RIGHT There's some truth to the notion that today's pickups are the basis for the hot rods of the 1990s. This Chevrolet S-10 gets a custom flame paint job, chrome wheels, and a lowered suspension.

It seemed for a while in the early 1980s that at every stop light there would be a young male driver sitting in a lowered mini pickup, windows down, the ba-boom, ba-boom base notes of the stereo vibrating everyone within 100 yards. And while the older guy in the sensible Chevy pickup might seethe at this display of youthful in-your-facery, there was something about all this do-your-own-thing truck culture that appealed. Maybe something could be done to spruce up the old half-ton Chevy . . .

And so a hot aftermarket was born.

While Ford trucks are the No. 1 sellers, it's indisputable that Chevrolet pickups are the favorites when it comes to customizing. One factor is that Chevrolet's restyling of its pickup line in 1988 created a vehicle with very appealing lines that seemed to lend itself better to body add-ons such as lower aero-skirts, front and rear air dams and other stylistic changes. The Ford F-series, with its more upright looks, was less of a candidate, though there were customized Fords.

Until the new Ford F-series appeared as a 1997 model, one very definite item that pushed the Chevrolet as the better base truck for customizing was its suspension. The Chevrolet used a traditional carlike kingpin/coil spring independent front suspension, while the Ford used an I-beam suspension. The Chevy suspension could easily be lowered by trading the coil springs for lower-profile springs. To lower the Ford required an all-new front suspension, which was expensive. Starting with its 1997 model, Ford switched to a kingpin/coil spring front suspension, which should put its pickups back in the customizing game.

Another factor – though less well documented – was that the Ford trucks seemed positioned in the marketplace as more of a work vehicle than a weekend plaything. Chevrolet marketing, while also stressing the work aspect of its pickups, seemed to push its trucks more as good recreational vehicles.

Until 1994, Dodge trucks were sold in so few numbers that aftermarket parts companies didn't find it cost effective to offer much to Dodge owners. With the exploding popularity of the new Ram pickup, that attitude is slowly changing. Nonetheless, by some industry estimates, Chevrolet accounts for as much as 80 percent of the custom market.

The market for all custom trucks is starting to

ABOVE Vivid graphics and lower body skirts combine with a front spoiler to give this Chevrolet S-10 a very sporty look. A paint job such as this could cost as much as $10,000.

ABOVE The grille on this Chevrolet C1500 has been replaced with a custom piece that hides the headlights. The grille is painted in the same pattern as the body, which has a camper shell mounted over the pickup bed. The raised hood indicates that the engine has been modified as well.

grow at an even faster pace as new vehicle dealerships start to stock trucks that are already customized. In recent years dealers have found they could make greater profits by installing custom parts themselves and factoring a hefty markup. Buyers go along with this because it saves them the time and trouble of getting the modifications made after taking delivery of the truck. Also, they can finance the entire package along with the truck, rather than having to shell out thousands of dollars after the sale.

So what goes into a custom pickup? Just about anything a buyer could want. Here are some of the more popular modifications:

LOWERED

This is the look that started with the small import trucks in California and has now been carried over to the full-size American pickups. There are several ways to achieve the lowered look, and varying degrees of lowering. On Chevrolets, the most popular change is to replace the front kingpin spindles with aftermarket units that lower the ride

height by 2 in. Combined with lower-profile coil springs, the modification can lower front ride height by as much as 5 in without changing the factory ride quality significantly. In concert with the lowered front, the rear leaf springs are relocated so that the rear axle rides on top of the springs. Called a flip kit, the repositioned springs can lower the rear of the truck by as much as 6 in.

On Fords the way to lower the front starts with replacing the factory I-beams with redesigned versions that lower the front of the truck by as much as 3 in. The addition of lower-profile springs can bring down the front an additional 2 in. At the back of the truck the process is much the same as with the Chevrolet. Dodge trucks are lowered in the same way as Chevrolet trucks are.

AERO SKIRTS

These are bolt-on composite body panels that can be attached along the lower rocker panels of most trucks. Non-functional, the skirts give many pickups the appearance of having been lowered.

REAR ROLLED PANS

This custom body piece replaces the rear step bumper on a pickup and gives it a smooth look at the back. The composite-material pan fits flush with the tailgate and the sides of the rear fenders, and is painted the same color as the rest of the truck for a Euro monochromatic look.

On Chevrolets a popular variation on the rear roll pan is a unit that relocates the rear brake lights from beside the tailgate to the rear roll pan in the form of four recessed lamps reminiscent of the Chevrolet Corvette. Metal plugs are welded into the sites of the original stoplights, sanded and painted the color of the body for a smooth rear-end treatment. Some pickup owners go even further and relocate the tailgate latch from the outside to the inside, creating a totally flush rear end.

A neat trick on some rear rolled pans is to conceal a trailer hitch behind the license plate recess. Just flip down the plate and your trailer receiving hitch is exposed and ready to take a trailer tongue and ball.

FRONT BUMPER MASKS AND SPOILERS

To achieve the Euro monochromatic look, many truck customizers fit a urethane or fiberglass mask over the chrome or black rubber factory bumper, and then paint the mask in the same color as the body. A more expensive alternative is to replace the factory bumper altogether with a painted metal bumper.

Another modification to the front is the installation of spoilers that run the width of the front bumper. These spoilers help enhance the lowered look of a pickup and also produce very slight improvements in freeway gas mileage.

BED COVERS, CAMPER COVERS, AND BED LINERS

These are the most common changes made on trucks by pickup owners.

In the case of a bed cover, it gives the pickup a finished look overall; some covers offer a little bit of security if items are stowed in the pickup bed. Bed covers run the gamut from vinyl tonneau covers that snap down over the pickup bed, to hard covers that swing up on hinges, to high-tech covers that can be raised electrically for access to the bed.

Along with bed covers, bed liners are popular options, and most manufacturers offer them as a factory option. Made of urethane or plastic, these liners slide directly into a pickup bed, many snapping into place. They protect the truck's finish from

BELOW The full-size Chevrolet pickup is a favorite of truck customizers in part because it is easy and relatively inexpensive to lower the suspension. This C1500 has a custom blacked-out grille, a front spoiler, fender flares, and, of course, a wild paint scheme.

Customized trucks are currently an undying trend, and let's face it, they sure are fun to look at! Just about everything from jazzy paintwork to big spoilers to serious tyres have transformed many of todays pickups into pretty enviable works of art. Appealing to today's youth, customized pickups are among the hottest automobiles you are likely to see.

ABOVE *This is definitely an all-American truck. A camper shell has been added to the back and the entire vehicle painted in a waving stars-and-stripes pattern.*

scratches and dents when items are tossed about. If the liner starts to look a bit scruffy, the fastidious owner can easily replace it.

Camper covers started out in the 1960s as a way to turn a pickup into a weekend-in-the-woods shelter. Now they have been made more stylish and some models can be used to give a pickup the look of a smooth-sided panel truck.

WHEELS AND TIRES

As with performance cars, trucks are being fitted with low-profile tires and chrome wheels.

For most full-size trucks, 16 in wheels mounted with rubber in sizes ranging up to 245/50 are good choices for a really hot look. Some customizers fit trucks with 17 in wheels and 40-series ultra-low-profile performance tires.

CUSTOM PAINT

At one time pickups were offered by manufacturers in strong, single colors – white, red, blue, black – but now the factories are turning out pickups in a rainbow of colors, ranging from purple through several shades of blue to black cranberry.

To match such colors the factories are adding their own stripes and graphics to enhance the sport image of their pickups. The Ford Ranger Splash is a prime example of a factory-finished truck that at one time could only have emerged from a custom shop.

Today, customizers offer paint schemes that challenge the imagination and dazzle the eye – a popular theme is a prism effect, with one color starting at the front and changing hues as it gets to the back of the truck.

SUPERCHARGERS

Want more power? Then pump it up!

A popular – though expensive – way to make a pickup special is to raise the hood and get to work on the engine. Since most truck engines have counterparts in cars – particularly the popular 5.7-liter Chevrolet V-8 – there are many aftermarket speed parts available that will still allow the engine to meet state and federal emission requirements.

One of the best ways to make a pickup more potent is to install a supercharger. A supercharger takes air and forces greater quantities into the engine's combustion chambers. More air means more fuel can be burned efficiently, and power output goes up. Unlike turbochargers, which use the engine's exhaust to ram air into the intake manifold, superchargers do not create high underhood temperatures. They run off the accessory pulley, making for easier installation and operation. Several aftermarket companies offer bolt-on supercharger kits that add as much as 100 hp to a stock pickup with no decrease in reliability and only a very slight penalty in fuel economy.

BELOW *This Chevrolet Sportside has been lowered, the grille has been replaced, and radical custom chrome wheels added. A supercharger has been added to the 5.7-liter V-8 as well.*

INDEX

Page numbers in *italic* refer to picture captions

A

aero skirts 184
airbags 105, 106, 109, 157
air-conditioning 40, 106
ambulances 11
art deco 16
Autocar 10

B

Baja 1000 *60, 65, 67, 162, 168–71, 169, 171*
bed covers and liners 185, 188
Benz 10
Bigfoot *162, 163–7, 163, 164, 165*
Bliss, Mike 179
Bonus Built 26
buckboards 8, 13
bumper masks 185
Busch Grand National 178

C

camper covers 188
camper units 34
Carroll Shelby 133–5
Chandler, Bob and Marilyn 163–4
Chevrolet 10, 11, *12,* 13, *15,* 16, 24–5, *35,* 46–83, 168–9, 177, *178*
  1980–1996 models 49–81
  4L60-E 73
  4L80-E 68, 82
  1500 Series 35, *71,* 178–9, *184, 185*
  2500 Series 35
  3100 Series 35
  3200 Series 35
  3500 Series 35, *70, 71, 82–3, 82, 83*
  3600 Series 35
  3800 Series 35
  Advance Design 25–6, *26,* 28, 31
  Apache 38
  Back Country 62, *63*
  Baja edition *65, 67, 69*
  Bel Air *40,* 42
  Blazer 19, 20, 50, 53, 91
  Bonus Cab 49, 54, 61, 74–7
  C10 *55*
  Cameo Carrier 31, 37–8
  Cameo S10 64, *65*
  Chevelle 42, 43
  Chevy Sport 50, 52
  Cheyenne 49, 50, 52, 62, 63, 64, 73
  C/K 9, 20
  C model numbers 35
  Corvair 42, 44
  Corvette 31, 81
  Crew Cab *34,* 49, 54, 61, 71, *71,* 74–7, *82–3, 82, 83*

Custom Deluxe 49, 52, 62
custom pickups *182,* 183, *183, 184, 185*
Deluxe cab 25–6, 29
Dooley *34, 71,* 74, 82–3, *82, 83*
Durango 52, 54, 62
EL 68, 71
El Camino 32, 40, *40,* 42–3, *43,* 59, 124
Extended Cab 53, *53,* 55, *57,* 61–2, *61, 81*
F-100 28–30
Fleetside *48,* 49, *49,* 50, *51,* 52, 53, *54, 57, 58, 61, 62, 63, 64, 65, 67, 67*
Fluid Drive 30
four-wheel-drive 39, *57,* 62, 63, 64, *72, 81*
fuel injection 57–9, *57, 67,* 78
Insta-Trac shifter 62, *67, 67*
K model numbers 35, 57, 70
LS *72, 81*
LUV (Light Utility Vehicle) 45, *45,* 51, 52, 61, 146
Malibu 43
Maxi-Cab 55, *57, 60*
Model 490 11, 17–18
model designations 35–6
Model T 11
Mountain Goat 21
S-10 (S10) 20, 45, 51–80, *52, 53, 57, 58, 60, 63, 65, 67, 69, 72, 73, 78, 79, 81, 91,* 128, 157, *182, 183*
sales figures 33, 48–9, *48,* 51, 52, 53, 57, 63, 64, 68, 71, 86
Scottsdale 49, 50, *51,* 52, *52, 57,* 62, 63
Series 10 35
Series 20 35
Series 30 35
Silverado 49, *49,* 50, 52, 57, 58–9, *58,* 62, 63
Sport 52, 54–5, *59,* 62, 63, 79
Sportside 61, *64,* 79, *189*
SS454 64–5, *67,* 68, 105
Step-Side 37, 49, 50, *50,* 53, *54,* 61, 98
Stovebolt Six 18, 33
Suburban 19, 20
Super Sport (SS) 78, *79*
suspension 48, 183
Tahoe 50, 54, *59,* 62, 67, 69
Task Force Service 31
Tech IV 59
turbocharger 49, 71
V-6 55, *57,* 58–9, 62–3, 64, 67, *71,* 73, *73,* 78, *78*
V-8 32, 33, 49, 51, 53, 55, 58, *58,* 63, 68, *71,* 80–1, *81,* 82, 189
Vortec engine 55, 80
Work Truck (WT) 64, 68
Z71 79
ZR2 78, *78*
Chrysler *20,* 28, 42, 118, 120, 124, 127, 136, 158

D

Dodge *see* Dodge
continuous running 67
convertibles 133, 135
Crosley 44
Cummins 125, 133, 141
custom pickups 48, 180–9
Daimler 10
Datsun 44, 146, 182
  see also Nissan
delivery cars 13
Diamond T 10, 17
Dodge 10, *10,* 11, *21,* 24, 27, 116–43, *118,* 177
  1980–1996 models 120–41
  1500 179
  Adventurer *34,* 121, 123
  Adventurer SE 121
  Adventurer Sport 121
  Base 136
  brakes 133
  Charger 124, *127*
  Club Cab *34,* 120, *130,* 134, 135–6, *138,* 141, *143*
  convertible 133, 135
  Crew Cab 120
  Cummins 125, 133, 141
  Custom *120,* 121
  Custom SE 123
  custom pickups 183
  D50 45, 121–2, 128, 146
  D100 *33,* 36, *36, 38,* 40, 126
  D150 120, 125, *125,* 126, *130*
  D200 36, 120
  D250 125, 126
  D300 36, 120
  D350 125, 126
  Dakota 120, 128–9, 133–6, 139–41, *141,* 158
  Dakota LE 129
  Dakota SE 128
  Dakota Sport 129
  Dooley *139*
  Dyna-Trac 123
  Fluid Drive 30
  four-wheel-drive 39, 120, *123,* 126, 127
  fuel injection 129, 133, 141
  Functional Design Era 30
  KC *15*
  Laramie SLT 139, 141, 142
  LT 138
  Macho Package 123
  Magnum 135, 141
  mini pickups 120, 121, 124, 128
  minivan 126
  Miser 125, *126*
  model designations 36
  Pilot House Safety Cab 27, *27,* 30

PICTURE CREDITS

Please note that the publishers have made every effort to identify the copyright owners of the pictures used in this publication; they apologise for any omissions, and would like to thank the following:

NICK BALDWIN: pp 6-7, 9, 11, 12, 13, 15, 18, 19, 21, 25, 26, 28, 29, 34 (3,5,6), 35, 40, 42, 43, 45, 116-117, 119 120, 121, 124, 125, 127, 152, 153, 157.

CHEVROLET: pp 34 (4), 46-83.

CHRYSLER: pp 10, 14, 16, 27, 31, 33, 36, 40-41 (c), 122-3, 126, 128-130, 132-143.

FORD: pp 2, 37, 84-115, 172, 173, 174, 176.

ALLEN LEVY: p38

MAZDA: 156.

MITSUBISHI: p 159.

NISSAN: pp 154, 155.

PETERSEN PUBLISHING: pp 20, 22-3, 24, 30, 32, 34 (1,2), 39, 41 (b), 44.

SCOTT D. JOHNSTON: pp 142-167, 180-187.

TOYOTA: pp 144-5, 147, 148, 150, 151, 160-161, 168-169, 170, 171.